OJIBWA CRAFTS

CARRIE A. LYFORD

R. SCHNEIDER, PUBLISHERS

Plate 1. Birch bark boxes embroidered with porcupine quills.

"Ojibwa Crafts" by Carrie A. Lyford (and other publications in the Indian Handcraft Series published by the Bureau of Indian Affairs, Department of the Interior) was formerly printed in the vocational education program of Haskell Indian Junior College in Lawrence, Kansas. In recent years, Haskell College has discontinued such programs and these books have thus, unfortunately, gone out of print. With this reprinting by Schneider Publishers, "Ojibwa Crafts" again becomes available for individual and classroom use. Our edition reproduces, as well as modern printing methods permit, the uncut version, only slightly diminished in size to reduce printing costs, with all the valuable original photos and line drawings intact. New cover pages have been added to include a full-color example of Ojibwa (Chippewa) beadwork from contemporary Minnesota artists.

Cover copyright © 1982 by Richard C. Schneider
ISBN: 0-936984-01-5
Manufactured in the United States of America

Published by:
    R. Schneider, Publishers
    312 Linwood Avenue
    Stevens Point, WI 54481

Related books available directly from R. SCHNEIDER, PUBLISHERS
or through your bookseller:
    Ewers: BLACKFEET CRAFTS
    Lyford: IROQUOIS CRAFTS
    Lyford: QUILL AND BEADWORK OF THE WESTERN SIOUX
    Schneider: CRAFTS OF THE NORTH AMERICAN INDIANS
    Underhill: PUEBLO CRAFTS

CONTENTS

ILLUSTRATIONS

Illustrations through the courtesy of:
(A)   American Museum of Natural History, New York City
(E)   Bureau of American Ethnology, Washington, D. C.
(D)   Denver Art Museum, Denver, Colorado
(H)   Museum of the American Indian, Heye Foundation, New York City
(P)   University of Pennsylvania Museum, Philadelphia, Pa.
(HDA)   Mr. H. D. Ayer of the Mille Lacs Indian Trading Post, Onamia,
        Minnesota
(I)   Bureau of Indian Affairs

Plate 2. Ceremonial dance Lac du Flambeau reservation. Drummers in center

THE OJIBWA IN HISTORY

SCATTERED throughout the wooded sections of the lake country in northern Michigan, Wisconsin, and Minnesota, and along the southern border of Canada are to be found the descendants of the great Ojibwa tribe of Indians, at one time the third largest Indian tribe in North America. Along the shores of Lake Huron, Lake Superior and the northern portion of Lake Michigan, as well as around the smaller lakes, the Woodland Ojibwa have continued to live since an early day. In Canada they are scattered from Eastern Ontario to Winnipeg, with some roving bands in the foothills of the Canadian Rockies.

Small groups of the Pembina band, the most westerly of the Ojibwa, have roamed from the northwestern section of Minnesota westward into North Dakota in the region of the Turtle Mountains and northward into Canada. A group known as the Nibowisibiwininwak settled in Saskatchewan. The Pic River group settled in Manitoba. These northern groups came in contact and mingled with the Cree and the Assiniboine. This branch was known as the Saulteaux, a name early given them by the French. Their proximity to the buffalo herds led them to adopt to a large extent the bison-hunting plains culture and they have been distinguished from the Woodlands Ojibwa by the title "Plains Ojibwa." Their handicrafts and manner of living closely resemble those of the other tribes of the northern plains and bear little resemblance to those of the Woodland Ojibwa.

Of the fifty or more language families in America the Ojibwa belong to the great Algonquian linguistic stock, one of the largest and most extended family groups. The Algonquian group includes tribes that have lived along the Atlantic coast from Quebec to Cape Breton Island, south to the coast of North Carolina, in the interior of Labrador, in the northern part of the drainage basin of the St. Lawrence, in the country of the three upper Great Lakes and upper Mississippi, and west into the plains of Saskatchewan and the upper Missouri. Throughout this territory a large number of related languages are spoken.

The Ojibwa are the largest subdivision of the Algonquian speaking stock. With the Ottawa and Potawatomi tribes, which also belong to the group, the Ojibwa formed a loose confederacy, frequently designated, in the last century, as the Three Fires.

The Ojibwa language is still spoken by the older members of the tribe and is used in the homes, but English has long been in common use by the younger generations in the schools and in contacts with the outside world. Among a few groups some French has been spoken since the days of contact with the French missionaries and fur traders. From the early days, inter-marriage and the common interest in trade served to perpetuate enduring ties with the French. A French dialect is used by the Turtle Mountain Indians in North Dakota.

The native name of the Ojibwa was "Anishinabe" (anishinabe, s., anishinabeg, pl.) meaning, first or original man (anic, first; nabe, male). The name Ojibwa was applied by their neighbors, probably as a descriptive term, and was later corrupted by the English into Chippewa, the name by which the tribe is commonly known today.

The origin of the word Ojibwa (O-jib-way) is thought to have been a corruption of "o-jib-i-weg" meaning "those who make pictographs" a word which was in turn derived from the expression "nind-o-jib-i-wa," meaning "I mark or write on some object." The engraved rolls or scrolls of birch bark which bore the records of the Midewiwin society of the Ojibwa were the nearest approach to written documents achieved by the Indians of the United States or Canada and were a distinctive feature of the tribal culture. Similar records on birch bark were kept by the Menomini, the Potawatomi, and the Ottawa.

An earlier explanation of the name, now considered incorrect, derived the word from "o-jib-ub-way" meaning "to roast till puckered up," referring to the tribal style of moccasins that has a puckered seam on the instep.

Another meaning given to the tribal name, Ojibwa, is, "he who sips soup or porridge with a sucking-in sound," which is regarded as a sign of appreciation.

The Ojibwa were described by early travelers as being generally tall, well-developed, good looking, active, intelligent, bold and independent. They had stately and easy manners and possessed real powers of oratory.

A total of 30,197 (1940) Ojibwa are estimated to be living in the United States, and 15,779 (1939) in Canada. Though early records of the population may be inaccurate, it is known that the members of the tribe have been increasing in numbers in recent years. Probably not more than 18.7% (1930) of the present number of enrolled Ojibwa in the United States can be regarded as full-bloods since inter-marriage with Europeans began with the first fur traders and has continued throughout the years. The French, Scots, and English intermarried with the Ojibwa during the fur trading period, extending through the eighteenth and the early part of the nineteenth centuries. Intermarriage with the Scandanavian and Irish began when lumbering was at its height, from 1850 through the eighties. Intermarriage with the Poles, Hollanders and various other nationalities followed. Intermarriage of the Ojibwa with Indians of other tribes has been increasingly common.

In the early part of the seventeenth century explorers found the Ojibwa living around the northeastern end of Lake Superior in what is now known as Sault Sainte Marie, in the Upper Peninsula of Michigan, and along the land lying opposite Madeline Island near the present town of Bayfield, Wisconsin. The country which they occupied was rich in marten, bear, otter, mink, lynx, racoon, fisher or pekan, and muskrat. Before the end of the century as the demand for furs by the Whites increased, the Ojibwa moved westward, across Lake Superior to the mainland on the far north near Isle Royale. It was here that Grand Portage (Minnesota) later figured in the romance of the fur trade.

The Ojibwa played an active part in the fur trade that developed across this section of the country, supplying the traders with pelts, fish, and game, in return for which they received firearms and other articles of European manufacture. The possession of firearms gave rise to a great change in their habits of living. They now entered into active conflict with neighboring tribes, driving the Iroquois off their land to the east, the Fox to the south, and the Sioux to the west. There was many a bloody battle between the Sioux and the Ojibwa in their struggle over the rich fields of wild rice in the lake country.

Plate 3. Map of Ojibwa reservation today.

OJIBWA RESERVATIONS

BY the year 1815 the Ojibwa had begun to make treaties with the United States Government. Between the years 1850 and 1880 their present reservations were set up and they have since lived at peace with both their White and their Indian neighbors. During recent years the management of the reservations has been grouped into a few large jurisdictions. In Michigan the Great Lakes Agency has supervision over the L'Anse (which includes Baraga), Las Vieux Desert, and Ontonagon Bands, all organized[1] as

the Keweenaw Bay Indian Community; the Bay Mills Band (organized); the Sugar Island group (unorganized); the Nahma group (unorganized), composed of both Ojibwa and Ottawa; and the Hannahville group. The last named is chiefly Potawatomi, but a few Ojibwa families have married into the group. In Wisconsin the Great Lakes Agency has supervision over the Lac du Flambeau, Bad River, Mole Lake, and Red Cliff bands, all organized, and the Lac Courte Oreille and the St. Croix Bands, unorganized. The Consolidated Chippewa Agency in Minnsota supervises the Fond du Lac, Grand Portage, Mille Lacs, Bois Fort or Nett Lake (including Lake Vermillion), White Earth, and Leach Lake Reservations, all organized together as the Con-

15

solidated Chippewa. The Red Lake Indians, an unorganized band, continue to live on a closed reservation[2] in northwestern Minnesota. On the Turtle Mountain Reservation, an allotted reservation[3], in North Dakota, a large group of the Pembina Band (unorganized) is now living.

The reservations set aside for the tribes were within the original territory occupied by the Ojibwa, and almost all of them contained regions of great natural beauty. On these the Ojibwa have continued to live, supporting themselves, much as they did in the past, by hunting, fishing, ricing, and berrying. The fur trade continued up to the middle of the nineteenth century. About that time the lumber companies were flourishing and remunerative work was to be obtained with them. As lumbering began to decline the Ojibwa took up farming on a small scale, but at no time have they been enthusiastic farmers, being by nature and long experience roaming trappers, hunters, and fishermen.

The Ojibwa were scattered in loosely knit bands or villages over a territory that extended more than a thousand miles east and west and approximately half as far north and south. Most of their homes were on heavily timbered plains, among low hills, near lakes or streams. Their woods abounded in pine, fir, and spruce in the higher portions, and in the lower sections, tamarack, willow, oak, poplar, ash, birch, elm basswood, and maple. Today much of their timber land has been cut over, though there are some federal and state forests on the reservations where the timber has been protected.

---

1.   The term **"organized"** is used to designate an Indian band or tribe that has adopted a constitution under the Act of June 18, 1934, commonly known as the Indian Reorganization Act. The "unorganized" band or tribe has not adopted a constitution under the Reorganization Act, but it may have an informal tribal organization and governing body, or council.

2.   A **"closed reservation"** is not open to homestead entries. It may or may not be alloted. The Red Lake Reservation has not been thrown open to White settlement nor has it been alloted to individual Indians. The entire area remains in tribal ownership.

3.   An **"alloted reservation"** has had the land divided up for allottment to individual Indians who have in the past been able to dispose of it without the consent of the tribe. Some of the land may still be tribally owned. An allotted reservation may or may not have been opened for White settlement by an act of Congress.

Plate 4.   Model of an Ojibwa lodge, illustrating construction.

OJIBWA LODGES

FOUR types of family dwellings (wigiwam, s., wigiwaman, pl.) were used by the Ojibwa—the domed and peaked wigwams for use in winter, and the bark house and conical lodge for use in the summer.

The domed wigwam (waginoǯan, s., waginoganan, pl.) had vertical sides of poles or saplings set in the ground and bent over in a series of arches. Encircling horizontal poles were tied firmly to the vertical poles at intervals with strips of green basswood fiber. Cattail mats were used for walls and roof. Sheets of birch, ash, or elm bark were laid over the upper mats to provide a waterproof roof. Both mats and bark were put on so as to overlap like shingles. The framework was permanent, the coverings could be carried from place to place. In the permanent camp sites the floor plan was rectangular. A circular form, however, was employed for the sweat lodges, menstrual huts, and temporary dwellings.

The peaked lodge (wigwassiwigamig, s., wigwassiwigamigon, pl., birch bark covered) like the wigwam was covered with cattail mats and sheets of birch or elm bark, but instead of being dome-shaped it had a long ridge pole

Plate 5. Peaked Ojibwa lodge, covered with birch bark.

connecting a series of A-shaped arches. The sides sloped straight to the ground.

The bark lodge (wanagekogamig, s., wanagekogamigon, pl.) was substantial and permanent, for summer use. It was a rectangular structure with a framework of pine, elm, or oak poles making the walls and peaked roof, and an outer covering of sheets of elm or cedar bark. It closely resembled the Long House of the Iroquois though the Ojibwa constructed it for individual families.

The conical or pointed lodge (nassawaogan, s., nassawaoganan, pl.) consisted of a framework of poles 10 to 16 feet in diameter on the ground and 6 to 10 feet high with a covering of birch bark, boughs, or cloth. The conical lodge resembled the tipi of both the New England and the Plains Indians.

A temporary lodge or shelter (jingobigan, s., jingobiganan, pl.) consisted of a conical framework of poles covered with fir, balsam, or other evergreen with the boughs pointed downward. This shelter was set up for short fishing or hunting trips. It would keep out the rain and was quite comfortable.

A smoke hole was provided over the central fireplace except in the case of the peaked lodge where the crossing of the central supporting poles left sufficient opening for the passage of smoke. The fire was built by laying

Plate 6.   Domed wigwam, covered with elm bark.

four logs on the ground, radiating from the central flame, like the spokes of a wheel. As each log burned it was pushed inward toward the flame. The flame was small, clear, and almost smokeless. Around the fireplace were arranged the bed, clothing, weapons, and other possessions of the family. The bed usually consisted of a pile of skins or blankets spread either on sprigs of spruce or hemlock which were strewn on the ground or on a mat laid on a platform. A skin of caribou or other large animal or a sheet of bark was hung at the entrance of the wigwam to serve as a door.

Most of the permanent lodges had a shelf or platform 18 inches or more in width raised about a foot above the ground, extending along one side to serve for a bed, chair, table, or work bench. During the day the bedding was rolled up and put away except for the mat, which was left to cover the sleeping platform, which now became a seat for family and guests. A central mat (anakan, s., anakanan, pl.) woven of cedar bark or reeds, was spread upon the ground to serve as a carpet.

A medicine pole was commonly erected near all permanent dwellings.

Plate 7.   A summer home of birch bark.

It was about 18 feet high and it usually carried the totem sign of the owner of the lodge or the sign of the spirit-guardian of the shaman or midé priests who performed the curing ceremony for which it was erected. To it was attached a sacrifice to the manitou, a term used to designate the mysterious and sacred powers of life. The sacrifice might take the form of a piece of calico, which at one time was highly valued because of its scarcity or of some other article that had high significance to the Ojibwa.

In times of peace, the eagle flag was planted in the ground at the head of the chief wigwam. It was made of feathers taken from the wings and tails of eagles closely woven together with basswood bark fiber. The quill ends of the feathers were put into the end of a pole that had been split with a flint. The end of the pole was then wrapped with sinew and bark. Having first been charred by fire the pole would stand for many generations.

Today some of the Lac du Flambeau Ojibwa who live at the old village have two poles about 6 feet apart in front of their houses. One is a soft maple pole bearing a white flag on which there is a bird or other totem. The other pole is a tall evergreen tree with only the top branches left on. Its presence indicates that a ceremony has been held there.

Plate 8.   A modern log dance hall.

In time the Indian lodge was replaced by the frame house (wakaigan, s., wakaiganan, pl.) though the old people continue to enjoy the lodge for summer residence. Singularly enough it is the winter mat house, the most difficult of construction, that is used today as a temporary summer shelter.

RECREATION

PROBABLY no tribe has been more favorably situated to enjoy wholesome sports than have the Ojibwa. With an invigorating climate and an abundance of woods, lakes, and streams they have always taken pleasure in hunting, canoeing, fishing, swimming, playing lacrosse and snow-snake, tobogganing, and snow-shoeing, which activities have contributed to their vigorous physique. Dances of various kinds were held on every important occasion.

A big, circular dance hall was constructed of logs. Several openings were left for windows. A central opening in the roof provided for the escape of smoke from the council fire. During more recent years the dance hall has been built of lumber and the roof has been shingled.

Plate 9.   Preparing framework for the Grand Medicine Lodge.

RELIGION

THE spiritual life of the Ojibwa centered around the Midéwiwin or Grand Medicine Society which prevailed throughout the Ojibwa country, though its form differed somewhat in different sections. It was a powerful organization which colored all aspects of Ojibwa life.

A large, mat-covered lodge known today as the Grand Medicine Lodge (midéwigamig, s., midéwigamigon, pl.) in which the rites of the midéwiwin were celebrated, was built in an open grove or clearing. This was a long wigwam built over a stout framework of saplings rigidly held together with other saplings placed horizontally, secured by a basswood bark cord at every crossing of poles. It varied in length from 100 feet to 200 feet, in width from 13 feet to 30 feet and in height from 7 feet to 10 feet. The apex was open. A covering of cattail mats and sheets of birch bark sewed together was provided for use in rainy weather.

Near the midéwigamig was erected a sweat lodge (abwesowigamig, s., abwesowigamigan, pl.) about 10 feet in diameter and 6 feet high in the middle with an opening at the top. It was constructed of saplings covered with birch bark. The sweat lodge served a ceremonial purpose during the Midewiwin observances.

The Midéwiwin songs, embracing the traditional history of the tribe, have been preserved on birch bark charts by a series of mnemonic symbols from which the songs were recited. The principles of ethical conduct formed a part of the teaching of the Society. Dreams, the phenomena of the natural world, and the desire for the attainment of long life colored many of the tenets of Midéwiwin. Admission to the Midéwiwin has always been a matter of great importance and attained with difficulty. Meetings were held once a year in the Midéwigamig to perform the initiatory and healing rites which were carried on by carefully trained and influential Midé priests or shaman, commonly called medicine men. There were several degrees of the order through which the members had to pass by initiation. Rattles and a sacred drum were used in the ceremonies. Every member had a "midé" bag which designated the degree to which he had attained. Among many groups the Society continues active today and its ceremonies are carefully observed, but the outside world has little knowledge of its activities.

During the latter part of the nineteenth century another religious ceremony called the Dream Dance came into prominence among the Ojibwa, and among some groups has since ranked in importance with the Midéwiwin ceremonies. It was primarily an out-of-door ceremony which took place about the first of July. A special dancing ground was prepared for the ceremonies which centered around a large elaborately decorated drum and a special calumet or sacred pipe with a catlinite bowl. The long stem of the pipe, which was the part held in reverence, was often carved, inlaid with metal or painted. Special keepers were appointed for the care of the pipe and drum between ceremonies and occasional offerings of tobacco were made to the drum.

DIET OF THE OJIBWA

B ECAUSE of the wide territory which they covered, living conditions and food habits of the Ojibwa varied within the tribe.

In most sections of the Ojibwa country fish, wild rice and maple sugar have always been staple articles of diet, as well as important in trade. All animals trapped for trade were eaten—moose, deer, bear, and rabbit. Ducks, pigeons, and other wild birds were relished. Wild berries such as red raspberries, huckleberries, cranberries, wintergreenberries, bearberries and other fruits, grains, a few edible roots and a variety of wild vegetables helped to give a varied diet. Corn, beans, squash, and pumpkins were cultivated in gardens by some of the Ojibwa before the coming of the White man. But the early Ojibwa were nomadic and slow to practice the cultivation of the soil and often in their primitive state they starved or were surfeited with the fluctuations of the food supply.

ACTIVITIES OF MEN AND WOMEN

IN addition to carrying on religious observances and following the war path, the Ojibwa men engaged in hunting, trapping, and fishing, thus providing a large share of the food supply for their families.

The Ojibwa women led busy lives erecting and furnishing the lodges and preparing the food and clothing for their families. In addition to their household labors they took part in the preparation of maple sugar and the gathering of wild rice, and carried on a variety of crafts in which their skill has always been recognized. The tanning of hides, the preparation of cords and twine, the making of mats, bags, and baskets of native fibers, the converting of birch bark into useful articles, and the quill work undoubtedly date back to prehistoric times. Yarn bags and sashes, bead weaving and bead embroidery, and the ribbon work borders on robes and leggings became a feature of their tribal crafts after the traders offered the yarns, beads, and silk to the ingenious craft workers. With the new materials brought by the early settlers, the Ojibwa developed new techniques in some respect closely related to their primitive craft methods.

PREPARATION OF MAPLE SUGAR
(Sisibakwat)

THOUGH there is no evidence of the aboriginal use of maple syrup and maple sugar their preparation has been one of the seasonal activities of the Ojibwa throughout the historic period.

Early every spring with the arrival of the first crow the Ojibwa moved into the "sugar bush" (sisibakwatokan, s., sisbakwatokanan, pl.) to prepare the maple sugar which entered largely into their diet as a seasoning for fruits, vegetables, cereals, and fish, as a delicacy when eaten alone, and as a summer drink when dissolved in water. Groups of relatives or friends staked off a portion of the maple forest as their portion of the sugar bush. There in a small birch bark lodge, supplies for the gathering of the syrup and the preparation of the sugar were kept from year to year. A framework of permanent construction was covered with bark each year to provide a large lodge. Here the members of the camp slept and the sugar making was carried on. The lodge was usually round, but if there were to be many in the camp a ridge pole was erected to give more room at the top and a larger lodge was built. Platforms were built into the sides of the lodge to be used both for sleeping and as a place for utensils. A long fireplace was built either within or without the lodge. Near it was erected a structure of stout poles from which the kettles could be hung.

About the middle of March, when it was time for the sap to begin to run, the women went to the camp to get things in readiness, then they brought their families and household equipment, and settled down for a month of hard work with happy evenings around the camp fire.

As soon as the camp was occupied, the maple trees (Acer saccharum Marsh) were tapped so that the sap could be collected. Tapping required some skill and was done by both the men and women. There were often two or three taps to a tree. As many as nine hundred taps were made at one camp. From these the sap was collected each day in bark pails and carried to troughs that had been erected at the doors of the lodges or put into the kettles where the boiling took place. The fires were kept up all night. In the morning the sap was strained. Originally vessels of bark were used and the straining was done through a mat woven of narrow strips of basswood bark. During later years iron kettles have been used and the straining has been done through burlap or through a threadbare white blanket preferably woolen. After the syrup was strained it was returned to the kettles for sugaring off. This required especial care. It had to be heated slowly until of the proper consistency, transferred to the trough, where it was stirred with a maple-wood paddle until it was granulated, then poured into the birch bark makuks. The thrifty Ojibwa woman had much carefully prepared maple sugar in mocock of various sizes for the family and in little molds and cakes for the enjoyment of the children. Ojibwa groups living near the maple forests continue to go to the sugar bush in the spring when the sap is running, but the supply of maple sugar in the Indian homes is much more limited than it was in the early days.

Plate 10. Gathering wild rice.

WILD RICE (Manomin) AND ITS PREPARATION

WILD rice [Zizania aquatica var. angustifolia Hitchc (Z palustris L)] grows in lakes, ponds, and slow-flowing streams in Wisconsin and Minnesota and in the Atlantic and Gulf States, in sloughs of the Mississippi River, and along the shores of Lake Ontario, Lake Erie, Lake Huron and Green Bay. Among the Indians of the wild rice district in Wisconsin and Minnesota rice has always been one of the staple articles of diet. Seasoned with maple sugar or combined with broth made from ducks or venison, wild rice is still much relished.

The presence of wild rice in the Great Lakes region was one of the causes of the constant warfare between the Sioux and the Ojibwa Indians, and it made possible the extensive fur trade carried on in that region by the provision of food for the traders and hunters.

Preparation of wild rice was one of the most picturesque activities of the Ojibwa and was carried on as a cooperative enterprise by a family or neighborhood group. The rice was gathered in the early fall just before maturity. Canoes were poled through the rice fields by women. With a pole or forked stick the kernels were knocked down from the stalks into the canoes, in the bottom of which blankets were spread.

Since the rice is gathered before it is mature it is necessary that it be cured or ripened artificially, so that the tenacious hull in which it is enclosed can be easily removed. This is done by spreading it on racks and drying it in the sun or over a slow fire or by parching or popping it in a large iron kettle over a slow fire, the men stirring it with a paddle meanwhile.

After being parched it is threshed to remove the hull. In the old days the parched rice was put in a skinlined hole in the ground, covered with a skin, and tramped down by the moccasined feet of the men. Fresh moccasins were worn for the purpose. Today an improved threshing machine, powered by an old Ford engine often is used for the purpose.

Then the rice was winnowed by the wind as the women shook a small quantity at a time in large, birch bark trays. The wild rice was stored in bags woven of cedar bark, a layer of hay placed over the rice, and sewed across the top.

Wild rice was also packed in the skins of animals, such as the raccoon and the fawn, in the webbed feet of ducks, and in birch bark mococks, and stored away in holes in the earth which served as storage caches. Today much of the work of gathering and preparing wild rice is done cooperatively and modern equipment is being used, but the work is still carried on under the trees as in the old days and birch bark trays are still in use.

HANDICRAFTS

THE Woodland Ojibwa made good use of all the natural products so richly provided by the woodland country in which they lived. All parts of the trees, shrubs, and grasses found a place in their material culture. Saplings were used for poles for the lodges. The bark of trees was made into baskets, boxes, and trays, and provided lodge and canoe coverings. Fibers secured from the bark were twisted into cords and ropes. Roots were used for sewing birch bark strips together, for binding canoes, for weaving baskets, for dolls, and for many articles necessary in daily life. Reeds, rushes, and bark fibers were woven into coarse mats for lodge coverings and finer ones to be used on the benches and floors. Pine needles were valued for their pleasing perfume and served as fillings for cushions or pillows for the bed. Dyes with which to color handicraft materials and ceremonial articles were secured from barks, roots, leaves, flowers, and berries. Maple sap gave one of the staple foods. Pine pitch and the resin from black spruce trees served to calk the seams and cracks in birch bark canoes and containers, rendering them non-leakable. Resin from the balsam tree and from the bark of the prickly ash, cherry and slippery elm, and herbs of all sorts were used for medicinal purposes. Thorns from the thorn apple were used as awls. Rushes were tied in small bundles and used for scouring purposes. The leaves of the bearberry and the inner bark of the red osier dogwood were smoked in pipes for pleasure. There is some evidence that before the coming of the White man clay had been used in the making of pottery.

The Ojibwa of the early days were gifted in the ways in which they put the products of nature to practical use. Well-tanned buckskins, delicate quill work, mats of golden cedar, and sturdy birch bark containers are left to tell the story of their skill. The ancient curvilinear designs and the simple geometric quilled patterns done in soft colors carefully combined, show a love of beauty and an artistic restraint that make their old handicraft articles worthy of study. The early Ojibwa kept their handicrafts at a high level of excellence and honored good workmanship.

Because of the many contacts that have always been maintained between the White people and the Ojibwa, in the lumber camps, in the hunt, and in summer sports, the handicrafts of the Ojibwa are probably more widely known than are those of any other Woodland tribe. Except to one acquainted with the characteristic features of the work of each tribe there is little line of demarcation between the handicrafts of the Ojibwa Indians and those of their woodland neighbors. The craft articles of the Ojibwa, the Menomini, the Ottawa, the Potawatomi, and the Winnebago all show many features in common.

Plate 11.   Ojibwa women making birch bark baskets (left) and preparing fibre for mats.

In spite of early and continued contact with White settlers the Ojibwa in Michigan, Wisconsin, and Minnesota have continued to practice many of their native arts through the years, and interesting examples of their handicrafts still can be found throughout the western woodland country. However, the Ojibwa living in the Turtle Mountains in the extreme northern section of North Dakota have intermarried with the French Canadians and have so completely laid aside their native crafts that they are almost unknown to the younger members of the group. In an attempted revival of native hand work, lessons in the crafts have been necessary for many of the adults as well as the children.

Today on the reservations in Michigan, Wisconsin, and Minnesota a few of the older women are to be found weaving cedar bark and rush mats and yarn bags, tanning hides, doing bead work for their ceremonial costumes, making moccasins for daily wear, and using willow, black ash, birch bark, and sweet grass in baskets of both ancient and modern design. The crafts produced and the techniques followed vary among the different groups and with the individual craft workers.

Since need for the articles for daily use and in ceremonial expression is not so great as formerly, the volume and quality of production of the handicraft articles is greatly affected by the monetary returns that can be expected. During the summer months the Indian homes in Old Village, on the Lac du Flambeau Reservation in Wisconsin, present a busy scene with the women working at their crafts. The roadside displays of finished work are attractive to the ever increasing number of tourists. Around Mille Lacs Lake in Minnesota for miles the roadside stands display birch bark work, moccasins, and other beaded pieces, with the Indian craftsmen fashioning additional articles nearby. Scattered throughout the lake country evidences of the perpetuation of the crafts are found, a single stand sometimes appearing on a little-traveled road. Unfortunately much of the work offered to the tourists is hastily and poorly made in the eagerness of the craft worker to secure profit from the temporary market.

A good steady market for the best Indian work has never been established, though many of the traders handle hundreds of dollars worth of Indian-made goods each year. The uninformed tourist is willing to pay a small sum for curios, and trivial, poorly-made articles, large numbers of which are sold annually in the tourist season. There are few who are sufficiently well informed to be willing to pay a fair price for the larger, better-made pieces representative of the old Ojibwa arts. Acquaintance with the best of the Ojibwa work would no doubt create a steady market among those who would enjoy and find use for articles of Indian construction. This would in turn stimulate the Indian women to higher standards of workmanship in carrying on their ancient crafts.

Plate 12.   Grave markers. (See page 38)

WOOD AND BARK IN CRAFT WORK

BECAUSE they were a forest people, wood and bark were the materials in which much of the craft work of the Ojibwa was carried on. Wood was worked into splint baskets, bows and arrows, brooms, frames for snow shoes, water drums, war clubs, canoe frames and oars, paddles, flutes, heddles, pipes, fish lures, cradle boards, invitation sticks, grave boards or markers, sugar troughs, balls, lacrosse sticks and other equipment for games. Simple designs were sometimes scraped or outlined with a sharp bone on these old wooden articles. At a later period a thin wire rod was used for the work. The outlined designs were blackened with smoke, or colors were rubbed into the lines of the design. Rubbed with the fresh root of the blood root plant the wood took on an orange shade. Some carving in the round and in relief is found on spoon handles, but this appears to be the exception.

At one time bowls, plates, spoons, and ladles were cleverly wrought from a burly section of the elm, maple and other hard woods, though burls were less used than in the south and west. In some sections wooden utensils are still being made and continue in use. Before the introduction of steel knives, the wooden utensils were made by charring and by scraping with bone and stone instruments. At feasts every man carried his own wooden spoon and bowl to which the food was transferred with a large wooden ladle from

Plate 13.   Wooden spoons.

the common cooking pot, a practice that continues to be followed on many of the reservations today with the tin pail and spoon.

Some of the Ojibwa men continue to show skill in wood work though the need of the bow and arrow and the wooden household utensils no longer exists. There is some demand for the bow and arrow, for reasons of sentiment or for use in archery clubs and pageantry, and a few wood carvers find a market for those which they make. In Wisconsin an open hunting season for the Indians when they can kill the deer with bow and arrow precedes the open season for shooting the deer with a gun.

Frames for snow shoes continue in demand and will probably be made for many years to come. While the making of the cradle board for general use ceased a generation or more ago, old cradle boards are still used. Flutes (pipigwan, s., pl.) of ash, cedar, and box elder no longer made by the lover to woo the maiden of his choice, can be secured from the skillful craftsman who has preserved the art. The carved family totem (bird or animal) is found on old graves, but is seldom erected at the grave today.

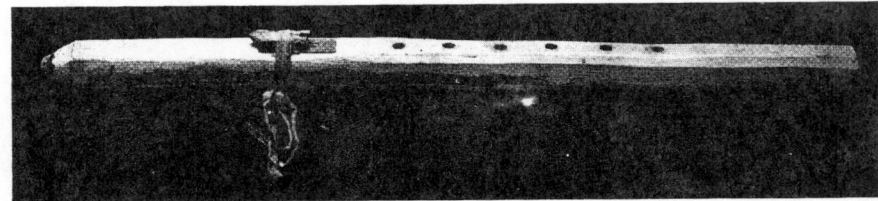

Plate 14.   Flageolet (Lover's flute).

Bows (mitigwab, s., mitigwabin, pl.) and
Arrows (pikwak, s., pikwakon, pl.)

The ancient bow of the Ojibwa was a flat piece of well seasoned hickory or ash, tapering at the ends. Iron wood and red cedar were also used for bows. Emergency bows were made of small trees, scraping off the bark and bending them. Before the White man's implements were available, the bows were made by the use of a wedge, flint, and fire. The length of the bow was determined by the distance from the point of the shoulder across the chest to the end of the middle finger of the opposite hand. A typical bow was about 48 inches long. The largest bows were about three fingers wide. Bows were made powerful enough to shoot an arrow through the side of a deer without difficulty at a distance of 50 paces.

Bows were decorated by coloring them with the juice of certain roots or by the use of a black mud. Lines were sometimes etched on the bow with a hot pointed stone and filled with red paint.

Bow strings were made of the sinew of moose or deer, of nettle stalk fiber, and of the skin from the neck of a snapping turtle. The nettle stalk fiber was waxed or rubbed with pitch to render it water-proof. The skin from the neck of the snapping turtle was cut off round and round to make a long strip which was twisted into a cord. It was said to be particularly valuable for the purpose, because it would neither stretch nor shrink and it lasted a long time.

The men spent every spare moment in the manufacture of arrowheads that a supply might be in readiness in time of need. The arrow was a shaft of reed or wood, feathered at one end and armed at the other with a head of bone, horn, or wood, or sometimes of shell or copper, but oftenest of flint, quartz, or slate. Some arrowheads were barbed and serrated. The arrowhead was fastened to the shaft with sinew. The Ojibwa arrows were not so long as those of the Sioux because the longer arrow was not convenient to use in the woods and also because the Ojibwa shot "from the knee," kneeling down to take aim. The Ojibwa arrow measured in length the distance from a little below a man's elbow to the end of his first finger. A blunt headed arrow was used for killing birds and smaller game and a pointed one for the fur bearing animals.

Feathers of the eagle and the hawk were tied on the arrow shaft with sinew. They were frequently dyed with bright colors. The kind of feathers used and their arrangement varied with the individual warriors. A good arrow would travel about 500 feet.

The arrows were carried in a quiver of stiff buckskin that was provided with a supporting band or strap and was frequently decorated with fringe and with designs painted in bright colors.

The strap of the quiver crossed the chest, passing over the right shoulder and under the left arm, the quiver resting upon the left shoulder so that it remained upright in any ordinary position assumed by the hunter. The arrows were easily available, they were drawn over the left shoulder with the right hand, while both arms could move freely across the body in front. The bow case was attached to the lower edge of the quiver, so that the bow was out of the way, but could be quickly drawn without releasing the arrows.

Wooden Brooms (tchigataigan, s., tchigataiganan, pl.)

At one time wooden brooms to be used in sweeping the dirt floors of bark houses, were quite generally made by the Ojibwa and other Indians of the eastern woodland. Today these brooms are not found among the articles made by the Ojibwa of Wisconsin and Minnesota because there it little use for them. The labor involved in their manufacture is great and they are so coarse that they are fitted only for rough work, such as cleaning yards.

Plate 15.   An Ojibwa baby on its cradle board.

The brooms were made of shag bark hickory [Carya ovata (Mill.) K. Koch] because it is tough, durable, and adapted to splitting in the manner desired. A 4 foot log, 3 inches in diameter at the base and 2¾ inches at the top, is used for a broom. Strips of wood about one-sixteenth of an inch thick and one-third inch wide are loosened from the lower end by use of a knife, and stripped free from the log for about 14 inches following the grain of the wood. A second row of strips was loosened from above these and turned down over them. These were beaten firmly against the first row, bound in place, trimmed until they were even, and hung in the sun to dry. A permanent binding of black ash splint was then carefully applied near the top and the broom was complete.

The Cradle Board (tikinagan, s., tikinaganan, pl.)

The first year of life was spent on a cradle board, by babies of earlier generations. The wooden frame for this cradle board was made by the men from a board about 24 inches long by 10 inches wide and ⅜ inch thick. Near the bottom of the board a curved piece of wood was attached, to confine the baby's feet. At the top a curved hoop or bow (agwingweon, s, pl.) flattened across the upper surface and notched at the ends, was tied or lashed to a wooden brace that projected at the sides. Some of the later cradle boards have the bow bolted on. The bow served to protect the baby's head and to support the blanket or the thin cloth used in summer to provide protection from drafts or flies. To the cradle the women secured a large piece of skin or a velvet sack or blanket so arranged as to hold the baby and to be laced up around it. Over this was tied a broad band to hold the baby in place. The band was usually attractively embroidered with quill or bead work. Moss or the down of cattail rushes was put around the baby for warmth. From the hoop that protected the baby's head were hung charms, coins, thimbles, bells and other play things. To the top of the board was attached a long leather strap or thong to be used as a tumpline which was passed around the mother's forehead when she carried the cradle on her back.

Dolls (odaminowagan, s., odaminowaganan, pl.)

Dolls were cut out of wood and bark or fashioned out of grasses, leaves, pine needles, or roots. The early dolls were crude and no features were shown. Especially sturdy dolls were made out of willow withes and of spruce roots. The root of the bullrush, tied with basswood fiber, was also used for dolls.

At a later period dolls were made of skins and cloth stuffed with spruce moss. They were usually dressed in the broadcloth or cotton costume that the women were wearing at the time and showed the prevailing type of bead ornamentation.

A doll was sometimes woven of cedar bark to serve as a container for wild rice. (See pages 96 and 161 for pictures of dolls.)

Drums (tewéigan, s., teweiganag, pl.)

The Midé drum or water drum used in the ceremonies of the Midéwiwin Society is a sacred instrument and is never used lightly. It is made from the trunk of a basswood tree. A section of the trunk is removed, hollowed out, and near the bottom a partition is made and glued in with pitch so that it is watertight. A hoop is driven on the bottom to make it more secure. A hole, fitted with a plug, is made on one side, and over the top, by means of a second hoop, is stretched a piece of skin. The hole and plug are for the purpose of introducing water into the interior of the drum to give the proper degree of sound. The drum is tuned by changing the depth of the water and reversing the drum so that the head of the drum is kept wet. The average drum is 16 inches in height, 12 inches in diameter at the bottom and 9 inches at the top. It is set up on feet when in use. The drum stick (pagaakokwan, s., pagaakokwanan, pl.) is a piece of ironwood 14 inches long and bent at the end, covered with deerhide or cloth. In some instances the drum sticks used in the midéwiwin ceremonies have symbolic significance.

Another piece of apparatus used in the Midéwiwin observances is the Ojibwa medicine drum or tom-tom which resembles a tambourine with both s i d e s consisting of skin stretched across a wooden frame. It is about 7 inches in diameter. In the center are a number of pebbles so that it serves as a rattle. The skins are painted red and black.

The drum used in the Dream Dance is made from a large wooden washtub with the bottom removed. The drum usually measures about 25 inches across the upper head, 23 inches across the lower head, and is 12 inches deep. Wet rawhide is laced tightly over each of the two ends so that the heads are both resonant. On the inside of the drum a small bell is suspended from a thong. This jingled pleasantly as the drum was being carried and while it was being beaten. The head of the drum is painted symbolically red, blue, and yellow.

The dance drum was low and placed directly on the ground, often without leg supports or decoration. Sometimes the drum was elaborately decorated. From five to nine men sat on the ground to beat it, using batons made of little elastic sticks on the end of which were attached pieces of leather or wads of cloth tied on by means of strings.

A small drum was made for use in the moccasin game.

MUSICAL INSTRUMENTS, AND BIRCH-BARK ROLLS CONTAINING MNEMONICS OF SONGS

Plate 16.   Musical instruments.

It is necessary to heat all drums except the water-drum in order to tighten the heads before using. The degrees and duration of the heat applied determines the tone of the drum. Sometimes ceremonies are interrupted to reheat the drum when it grows slack with beating. Another drum may have been heated in readiness for use during this emergency.

The Grave Marker or Grave Post (adjedatig, s., adjedatigwin, pl.)

Burial grounds were held in great esteem by the Indians. The early graves of the Ojibwa were covered with heavy hewn logs. Near the grave, upright poles, 4 to 6 feet high, were erected. At the tops of the poles strips of red or white cloth were attached. At one time a grave board or marker was placed at the head of the grave. The marker was a board or plank of cedar or other wood on which was carefully carved the family totem sign and other symbolic designs that indicated the number of war parties on which the deceased had been and the number of scalps he had taken. The symbol which showed the totem of the deceased was inverted to indicate death. (Page 30)

According to their oral traditions the Ojibwa were first divided into five chief totem clans. Other clans arose by sub-divisions, increasing the total

Plate 17.   Ojibwa burial ground with covered graves.

number. Each totem clan had a distinguishing sign or symbol taken from some familiar living object by which it could be identified. The totem clan name which descended from father to son was usually that of some animal, bird, or fish that could be represented by a crude drawing or design. In 1852 there were 21 of these totem clans bearing the following names: crane, catfish, loon, bear, marten, reindeer, wolf, merman (a fabled marine creature half fish and half man), pike, lynx, hawk, eagle, rattlesnake, moose, black duck, goose, sucker, sturgeon, white fish, beaver, and gull. Other clan names have been recorded at later times. Th drawings or signs that represented the names were used by the members of the clan on important occasions such as declarations of war or of peace,and on grave posts.

During more recent years throughout the Ojibwa country there prevailed a custom of erecting small houses (tchibégamig, s., tchibégamigon, pl.) over the graves. The first houses were of birch bark. Later they were made of lumber. At one end was a small opening or window below which was a ledge on which food, offered as a sacrifice, could be placed. Above the window a design was often painted. On some of the modern grave houses a realistic floral design has been used.

Pipes (opwagan, s., opwaganan, pl.)

Pipes held an important place in both the social and ceremonial observances of the Ojibwa. They were two classes, those for common, daily smoking, which were used individually, and those for ceremonial purposes, when only one was smoked and passed around the group. For the council or ceremonial pipe known as the "peace pipe" or calumet, a real reverence has always been felt. The pipe bearer was regarded as next in importance to the war chief. The stems and bowls of the pipes that were used for ceremonial purposes were often elaborately decorated. Special bags in which the pipes were to be kept, were embroidered by the women with handsome quill and

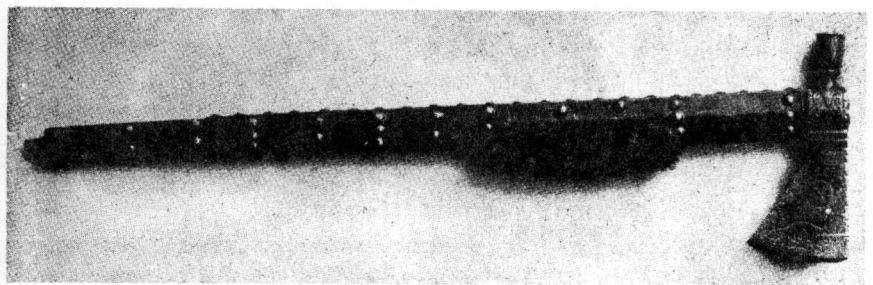

Plate 18.   An Ojibwa pipestone calumet (pipe) shaped like a tomahawk.

39

bead designs. Both the men and women smoked, the women sometimes using a miniature stone pipe.

Pipes used by the Ojibwa have been made of wood, stone, and metal. The wooden pipe bowl, made from the knot of a tree was sometimes decorated with an incised or carved design, or lined with metal, or provided with a metal tip. On some of the pipes there is a projection beyond the bowl, but this is not so long as is the projection on many of the Plains pipes.

Soapstone, limestone, black slate, sandstone, greenish gray steatite (artificially blackened with soot from pot bottoms), lava, granite, hematite, argillite, serpentinous rock, and pipestone have all been used by the Ojibwa for making pipe bowls.

Pipestone or catlinite found in the southwestern part of what is now Minnesota, has received the name of catlinite from George Catlin, the noted Indian painter, who brought the stone to the attention of mineralogists about 1839 though it had long been in use by the Indians. The color of the Minnesota pipestone varies from light gray to pale and dark reds. Pipestone, when first quarried, is quite soft so that it can be easily carved and polished with the most primitive of stone knves. With exposure to the air the pipestone becomes hardened and durable.

Metal pipes have been made of brass, iron, cooper, and pewter. After the coming of the White man metal was used to mend old stone pipes. Later the Plains Indians enhanced the beauty of their stone pipes by inlays of metal using lead, silver, and pewter in straight line designs or in more elaborate patterns on the bowls and stems of smooth black or dark red stone. Designs used in the decoration of pipes were said to have been suggested by dreams that came to the owners of the pipes. The Ojibwa may have obtained their more elaborate pipes from the Plains Indians.

The stem was the most important part of the Indian pipe. It often had ceremonial significance. The term "calumet," originally applied to the stem of the sacred pipe, is today used quite generally to designate the entire pipe. Most pipes for daily use were provided with two or three stems. Pipe stems varied in length from eighteen inches to four feet. They were usually made of wood, most generally of ash, and carved in rings or in a spiral form or with an elaborate open work pattern. A plain wooden pipe stem was sometimes scorched to give it a brown color, and then decorated with brass-headed tacks. Eagle feathers, hair, porcupine quill work, beadwork, and other trimmings were used to decorate the ceremonial pipes.

In the modern times the Ojibwa smokes commercial tobacco (assema, s.) in his pipes, but formerly he used native tobacco which was being grown as early as the seventeenth century. The native tobaccos were harsh, so they

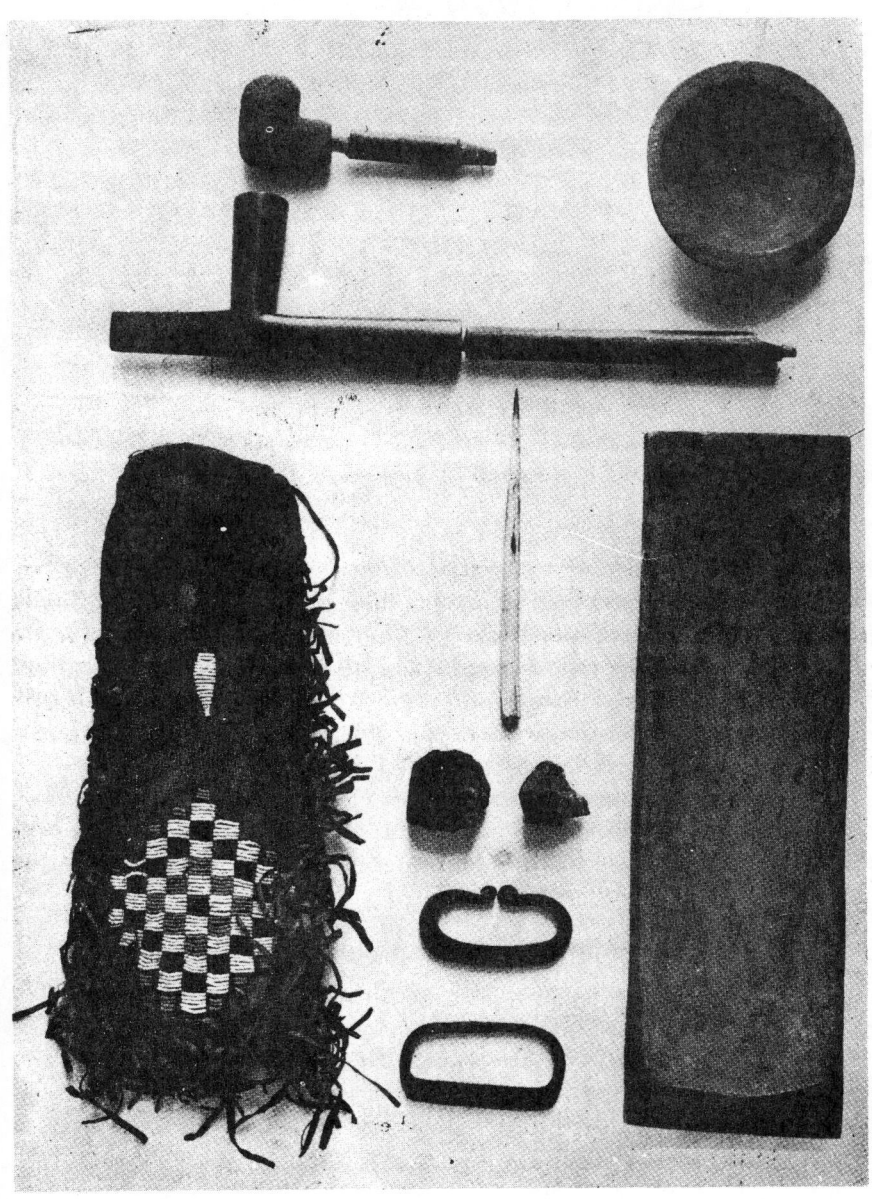

Plate 19.   Wooden dishes for mixing tobacco, pipe cleaners, beaded tobacco bag, woman's pipe (small), man's pipe (large)

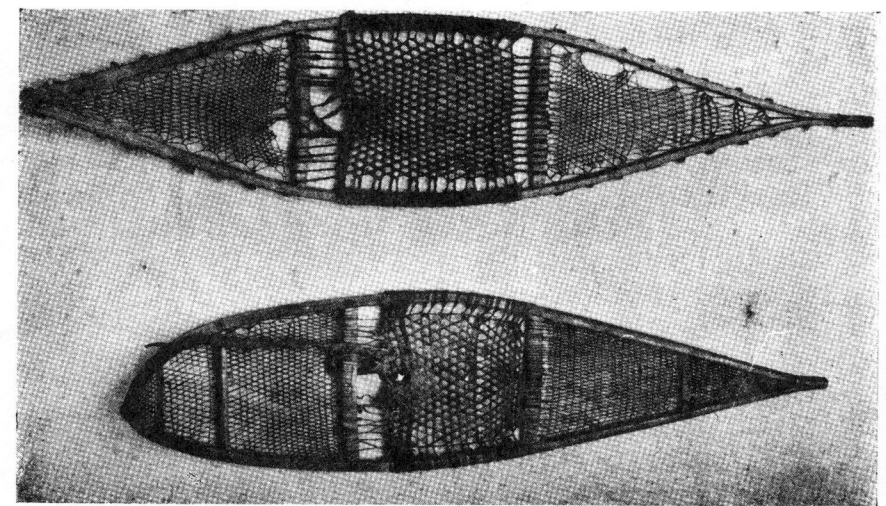

Plate 20.   Snow shoes.

were usually combined with a mixture of dried leaves and bark called kinnikinnik. The leaves and bark of sumac (Rhus glabra L.) red willow (Cornus Amomum Mill.) or red osier dogwood (Cornus stolonifera Michx.) and of other plants were commonly used in this mixture. The bark was scraped off in ribbons and dried on a special wickerwork, fan-shaped drier over a small bed of coals that was separated from the campfire. Such mixtures have continued in use up to recent times.

Tobacco was thought to have been the gift of the divine powers. It was the custom among aboriginal tribes to offer tobacco as a sacrifice to the spirits which they believed controlled their destinies. Tobacco smoking played a part in the Midéwiwin ceremonies.

Snow Shoes (agim, s., agimag, pl.)

Snow shoes were an essential part of the equipment of the Ojibwa because of the heavy snows and the long hunting trips which were necessary in winter. Oval or bearpaw snow shoes (so named because of their shape) were worn by the women. Long snow shoes with a pointed toe and heel were worn by the men. The toes were turned up when the shoes were to be used by hunters in the woods.

In the bearpaw snow shoes a simple type of netting or false weaving filled the frame. An elaborate hexagonal weave was used in the netting on the long snow shoes. Snow shoes were made with a wooden frame, usually of

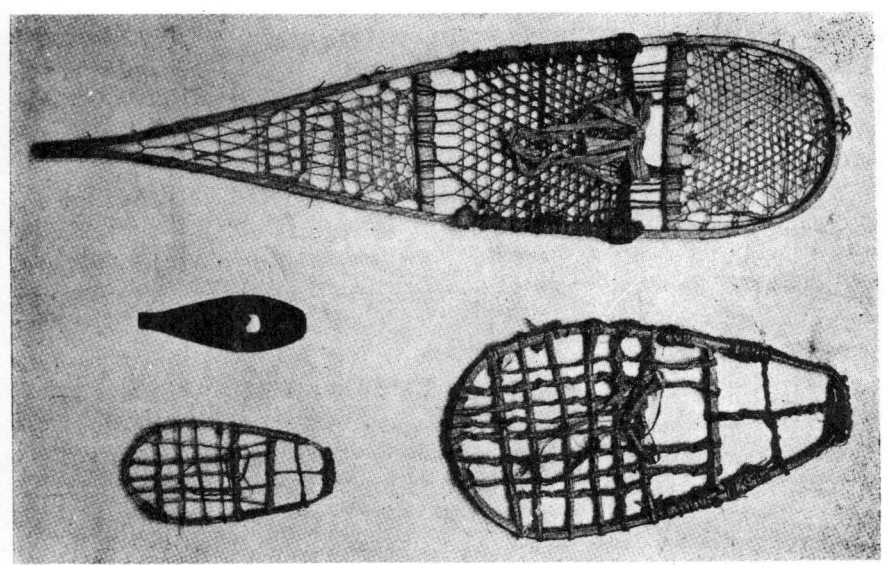

Plate 21.   Snow shoes—pointed and bear paw.

ash, strengthened by one or more crosspieces. To make the frame, strips of green ash (Fraxinus sp.) were rendered pliable by heating over fire or were steamed to soften the sap so that the wood could be bent to the required shape. Narrow strips of rawhide of the moose or deer, called babiche by the French, were used for the netting (assabikéwin, s., assabikéwinag, pl.) within the frame. In the old days the hide of the caribou was used. It was valuable for this purpose because it did not stretch or shrink when wet. After the introduction of the horse by the White man, the hides of the horse were used to some extent. Sinew and native twine were also used for the finer netting at the ends of the snow shoes, which was inserted through the frames. The coarser and more open netting under the feet was wrapped around the frames which were often protected by a piece of red flannel. A bone or wooden needle with the eye midway of its length was used in making the netting A piece of rawhide or leather was fastened on the netting where the feet rest. A leather thong carried through the netting was wrapped across the instep from the front to attach the snow shoe to the foot in hinge fashion. The heel was left free.

Plate 22.   Spreading fish nets to dry.

PREPARATION OF CORD AND TWINE

NATIVE cord and twine (biminakwanens, s., biminakwanensan, pl.) were among the most important articles in the economic life of the Ojibwa, for they were used in many of their crafts. Cord was made from the stalk fiber of the false nettle [Laportea canadensis (L.) Gaud. (Urticastrum divaricatum)], and the bark of the basswood (Tilia americana L.) white cedar (Thuja occidentalis L.) and slippery elm (Ulmus fulva Michx.). Deer sinew and strips of rawhide were also used as cord.

Nettle Fiber and Its Uses

The nettle weed or false nettle (masan, s., masanag, pl.) often referred to by the Ojibwa as a thistle, grows abundantly in the lake country. The nettle stalk (masánashk, s., masánashkon, pl.) is made up of long fibers that are very strong. The stalks were cut in October, tied in bundles, and hung to dry. When they were to be used the woody stalks were rotted and then heckled or beaten with sticks to loosen the fibers. If the rotting process is continued too long and the fiber is rotted, it cannot be used. The fine, white, shredded fibers thus secured were spun without the aid of a spindle. Two strands were taken in the right hand and rolled together against the thigh until they twisted themselves into an even cord. More fibers were added as needed. The cord varied from the thickness of a pack thread to a twine about three-sixteenths of an inch in diameter. In appearance the nettle weed fibers closely resemble cotton, but they are longer and stronger.

The nettle fiber cord was firm and strong and was used for sewing, and for fish nets, snares for rabbits, and traps for the otter. The finest of the nettle fibers were at one time woven into a cloth that was used for women's underskirts. The fiber was also woven into large flat bags on which designs were worked out with dark brown buffalo wool.

Basswood Fiber Cord

Basswood fiber (wigob, s., wigobin, pl.) comes from the inner bark of the basswood or American linden tree (Tilia americana L.). Various methods were used in preparing it for twine. In the spring and early summer when the sap is flowing, the bark can be easily peeled off the young trees in long sheets. It is then cut lengthwise in strips about 4 inches wide and laid among the reeds at the edge of a lake or pond and soaked in the waters for about ten days, after which the rough outer bark can be easily detached and the soft yellow fiber or inner bark pulled off in shreds or strips less than an inch wide, wound in coils, and hung to dry.

If it was not to be made into cord until a later time, the shredded bark was stored away until needed. When the cord was to be made, the bark was moistened and separated into layers. When wet the fiber can be readily bent and tied, but it is easily broken when dry. If a very strong cord was desired, the bark was folded into small bundles and boiled for an hour or more. Wood ashes were sometimes added to the water in which the bark was boiled. When the fibers would separate readily they were pulled apart in the widths desired. The width of the fiber determined its strength. The stiff fibers were then worked in the hands until soft and ribbon-like. To secure a softer fiber they were drawn through a hole driven in the dried shoulder blade or the pelvic bone of a deer. The fibers were drawn back and forth until softened.

When a woman was ready to make the cord, she sat down on the ground, drew two strands through her mouth to moisten them with saliva, spread them an inch apart on the right side of her leg at the thigh or slightly above the ankle and rubbed them with the palm of her hand so that the strands each became twisted separately, then with a reverse motion of the hand they were twisted together. To gain length, two more strands were then moistened in the mouth, and added to the twisted fiber so that they over-lapped, and the twisting process was continued. The cord was spliced so per-fectly that the joining was invisible. Water was kept at hand to moisten the hands and the strands while the cord was being made.

Cord from the inner bark of the cedar and the slippery elm was prepared in the same way, but the bark from the slippery elm required no soaking.

For some purposes the fibers were used without twisting. The untwisted bark fibers served as thongs and were used for tying sinkers to fish nets, binding packages, and for sewing tops on bark and woven containers. "Rice twine," used for tying sheathes of wild rice in the field, was prepared by tying narrow strips of the untwisted basswood fiber end to end before it had begun to dry. The strips were wound in a ball in such a way that the ball could be unwound from the middle.

Cord made from bark fibers served many useful purposes. In addition to its use in the textile arts, in sewing birch bark receptacles, and as a warp in rush mats, burden straps, and bags, the basswood fiber was used in tying together the poles of tripods employed to support the kettles in cooking, in tying house poles together, in attaching floaters and sinkers to fish nets, in netting for snow shoes, and making fish traps, nets, and lines. Today machine-made twine is used for the fish nets and for most other purposes.

BIRCH BARK (Wigass) WORK

THE white birch (Betula papyrifera Marsh.) grows throughout the northeastern part of the United States from Long Island on the Atlantic Coast westward to the Rockies, skirting Nebraska and running along the international border and adjacent parts of Canada, and northward from Newfoundland to the Mackenzie River Basin and into Alaska.

Though birch bark has been available to all the Woodland Indians, the use of birch bark in their material culture has been restricted to the Canadian tribes and to a few of the tribes bordering on the Great Lakes to the south. It has always been one of the most important resources of the Ojibwa, and has played an important part in their material culture. Because of its importance to them, the Ojibwa are often thought of as the "Birch Bark Indians." The bark is made of layers of different thickness. It can be torn crosswise almost as straight as cloth. It is wind and waterproof, very tough and durable, and almost proof against decay.

The thickness of a piece of birch bark determined the use to which it could be put. The "spring peeled" bark, often referred to as winter bark, is heavier and harder to remove than the summer bark, and very durable. That coming from the largest trees shows from six to nine distinct layers and is strong enough to be made into canoes. Some of the bark is as thin as tissue paper and tough enough to use for wrapping packages. Between these extremes there are different grades of thickness in the bark as it comes from trees of different sizes. If bark was removed from the trees without injury to the cambium layer in which the sap flows, the life of the tree would continue and in time a new layer of the bark would cover the cambium layer.

When great sheets of birch bark were needed for canoes and other larger articles, the trees were felled before the bark was removed. The bark was then cut the desired length and split to remove it from the tree.

If small pieces of birch bark were needed, only the outer bark was removed from the tree. Thin pieces could be removed if care was exercised in cutting it. An incision was made down the length of the tree as high as a woman could reach. The bark was then pulled off and rolled or folded for storing. As many as one hundred sheets of birch bark were piled in one pack (Apakwas—birch bark rolls), tied together with basswood strips, and carried by a strap on a woman's back to be stored in her home.

The Ojibwa were able to remove large quantities of bark without destroying their birch trees because they had learned the most favorable time for stripping the trees without harming them. The time varied in different localities. They gathered the bark from the time the leaves of the birch tree were completely unfolded until the end of July, before it was set and while it could be easily peeled from the tree. Gilmore speaks of the time for gathering bark as being the time "when the wild raspberries began to ripen." Elm bark, which was also used for roofing lodges, could be secured most satisfactorily at the same time.

The women made transparencies by folding thin sheets of birch bark

Plate 23.   Birch bark torches.

and biting them in such a way that they showed symmetrical patterns when unfolded and held to the light. A flambeau or torch of birch bark was used by the hunter for "shining" the deer and was attached to the bow of the canoe to provide light when fishing at night. Slender torches, stuck in the ground, were also used by the women when working around the camp after dark. Motifs for quill and beadwork patterns were cut out of birch bark and kept on hand for future use. Storage boxes of various sizes, the "quick pack," sap buckets, and dishes of birch bark were made in great numbers. Large thick sheets of birch bark cut in the early summer were used for canoes and for lodge coverings. Splints made of birch bark were used on fractured limbs. Birch bark was used to wrap the bodies of the dead and to cover graves.

Midé Rolls

The men made charts and pictures that served as memory-aiding devices by engraving on birch bark a system of symbols which they carried almost to the point of true hieroglyphics or picture writing before the coming of the White man. Over two hundred characters were used in their picture writing.

During the spring months the outer bark was peeled from the trunk of the birch tree and cut in strips of the width and length desired for the rolls on which the records were to be made. A roll was 30 inches or more in length and about 12 inches wide. The ends of the rolls were rounded or strengthened

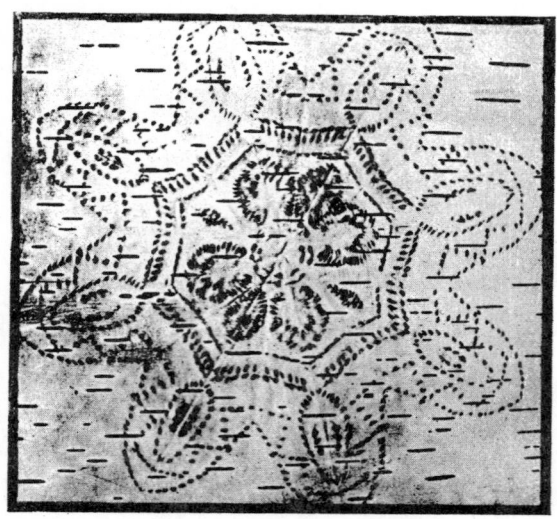

Plate 24. Bitten pattern on birch bark.

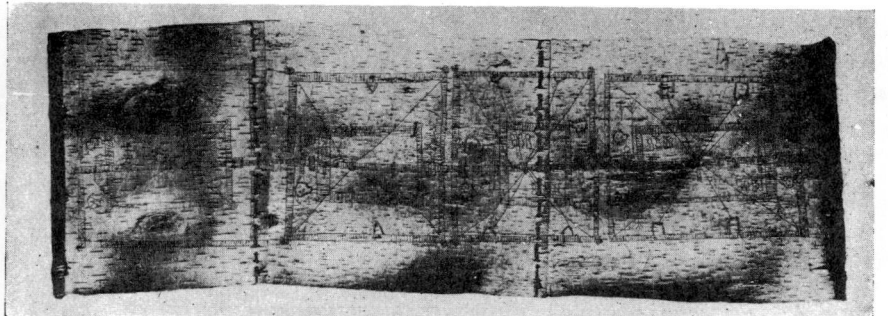

Plate 25.   Birch bark scroll or midé roll.

by strips of wood. one being securely fastened on each side. Pictograph-ic characters and mnemonic marks were traced on the inner surface of the bark with a sharply pointed instrument, usually of bone or stone. Large cir-cles corresponding to the number of the lodges or degrees of the Midéwiwin were sometimes traced on the outside of the rolls. The birch bark rolled up after drying and it was necessary to heat it in order to straighten out the roll for examination.

Mats of Birch Bark (wigwassapakwei, s., wigwassapakweiag, pl.)

Mats of birch bark to be used as a covering for the wigwams or lodges were made from narrow strips of bark (the width determined by the size of the tree). The mats were 12 or more feet in length. The sheets of bark were overlapped and sewed together with untwisted basswood fiber. They were strengthened at the ends of the completed mat by attaching nar-row strips of cedar about ¼ inch thick to keep them from tearing. When used on the lodge, the mats were placed horizontally and were fastened in place at one corner by a basswod cord. The mats could be instantly rolled up in compact form for removal. When put in place on the wigwam roof they were arranged like shingles to shed water and projected like eaves.

Birch Bark Canoes (wigwass-tchiman, s., wigwass-tchimanan, pl.)

Because of the many lakes and streams in the woodland country, the Ojibwa depended to a great extent on canoes for transportation when fishing, hunting, trading, or going on the war path. The typical Ojibwa canoe was of birch bark. A good birch bark canoe would last a man for one year. Old canoes were kept for home use and light trips.

Canoes varied in size from small river canoes that were handled by

Plate 26. Making a birch bark canoe.
a. Smoothing the ground with sand to conform to the canoe bottom.
b. Heavy stones holding the bark for the bottom of the canoe in position.
c. Stakes driven in the ground to determine the slant of the sides and the width of the beam of the canoe.

two men to the Montreal or voyageurs canoe that was 35 to 40 feet in length. This large canoe was used in traveling the Great Lakes. It was handled by from 8 to 10 men although it could carry more paddles and less baggage or cargo if greater speed was desired. A smaller canoe 24 feet long, commonly called a four fathom boat or north canoe, was used on the inland lakes and rivers. It could use a crew of 8 men although only 4 or 5 men were used when carrying passengers and cargo.

The making of a birch bark canoe required much skill. When a canoe was to be built heavy birch bark was collected in late June or July (when it would peel off most easily), rolled up, and laid away in the shade. Before shaping the canoe, strips of white cedar (Thuja accidentalis L.) or other straight-grained green wood were carefully split and whittled into the required sizes to form the ribs, sheathing, thwarts, and gunwales for the top of the frame, and were placed in the water to render them more flexible. Poles and stick were brought to the proper length by the use of fire.

All measurements for a canoe are calculated by distances between various parts of the human body. The correct depth of a canoe amidships was the distance between the elbow and thumb. The right distance between the ribs was the span from the little finger to the thumb. Black spruce root was used for measuring.

When the canoe was to be started, towards evening, or at any time when the day was cloudy, the bottom pieces of bark were placed in position, overlapping a few inches in the middle where they were to be joined. If a single length of bark was not available, two or three pieces of bark were used, as necessary. Stones were laid on the bark to hold it down, and a temporary bottom frame, approximating the width of the canoe at the bottom and pointed at both ends, was then applied. Stakes were then driven into the ground, nine or more to a side. They were placed at intervals to approximate the length and width of the canoe and were arranged to flare outward slightly.

Up to this point the work was carried on by the men. The next step was performed by the women. They made slashes or gores on each side towards the ends where the canoe begins to narrow, and sewed them with the fine roots of the spruce [Picea rubra (Du Roi) Dietr.],tamarack [Larix laricina (du Roi) Koch] or the jack pine [Pinus banksiana Lamb. (P. divaricata Gordon)]. Before using the spruce root for sewing, the women split the fibers to a suitable size and rendered them flexible by steeping them in fish broth.

The men next laid the upper lengths of bark alongside, measured them by trial, then placed them in position. The bottom pieces were then scored along the bottom with an ax where they were to be creased for the taper to bow and stern, after which both the upper and lower barks were

Plate 27. Making a birch bark canoe.

d. The gunwales placed lengthwise and the bark sewed in place.

e. An end view after the gunwales have been installed.

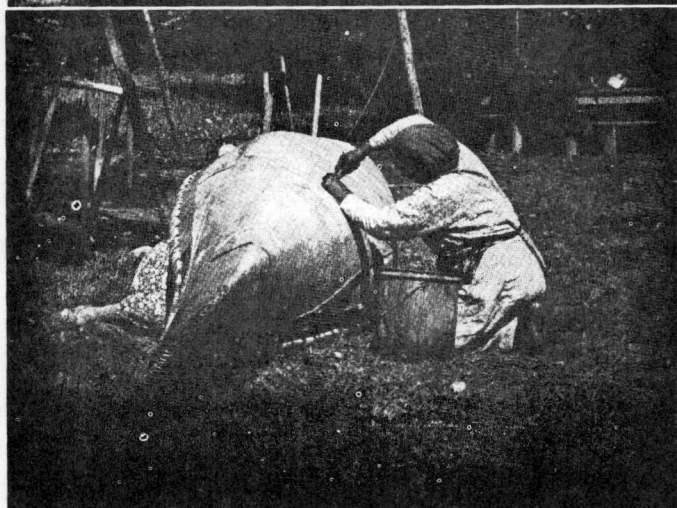

Plate 28. Making a birch bark canoe.

f. The ribs and f l o o r i n g from green cedar saplings m u s t b e soaked in water three days before the ends are inserted between the gunwales.

g. Seams in the bark a r e sealed with spruce pitch.

pinched together by stakes driven closely and tied at the top. An inner frame (or "inside gunwale") giving shape to the upper edge of the canoe, and having exactly the right taper and curve, had been prepared beforehand, and was now placed between the upper edges of the bark and sewed closely and firmly to them. Pieces of cedar, bent to the approved shape of bow and stern, were placed between the barks at the ends of the canoe, and the bark trimmed to conform to those in outline, then sewed to them with spruce root. In all cases the sewing was done by the women. Stitches of uneven length were often employed, particularly around the ends, to prevent the bark from splitting. After being sewed the gores and laps were well stuck together with a clear spruce gum that had been boiled a little to thicken it. All laps had their outer edges running backwards or towards the stern, so as not to obstruct the motion of the canoe.

The bottom frame, which was merely temporary, was then removed, The ribs taken from the water, bent to shape around the knee, cut to length, and driven into place with a mallet. Other thin strips of cedar, 3 or 4 inches wide, were driven between the ribs and bark as the work proceeded, for the purpose of forming a protective flooring and siding. The canoe, particularly at this stage, was kept well moistened both inside and out. The placing of the ribs and sheeting proceeded, generally speaking, from the ends to the center. Cross pieces, to keep the top spread, were hammered in at every second rib. The ribs were a couple of inches wide and about the same distance apart. When the insertion of the ribs and sheeting had been completed, a general correction was given to the shape of the canoe by tying it between stakes and exposing it for a while to the sun. When the canoe was completed, it was taken from the frame and inverted, preparatory to being gummed with pitch.

By the time the canoe was put together, the women would have the spruce gum ready to gum the seams to make them waterproof. The spruce gum was obtained from trees that had been gashed the year before, boiled a little while to thicken it, and mixed with powdered charcoal for ornamental purposes. The bottom seam was coated with clear gum, and pegged, not sewed. The last step in canoe making was to attach a top gunwale strip by tying or binding it on with spruce root.

The Ojibwa used an extremely simple canoe paddle made of clear c e d a r or other light wood. It was about 4 feet in length of which nearly one half was devoted to the blade which varied in width from 4 to 6 inches. Two paddles were used in the small canoe, one in front and the other in the stern. The paddler knelt or sat rather low, the toes turned inward and bent backward beneath the body. On a long journey a pad of leaves or clothing was placed beneath the legs for comfort.

Plate 29.   The finished canoe ready for its maiden trip.

A birch bark canoe can be made in from ten days to two weeks if all the materials have been prepared and are at hand. The bark for the covering and sewing, the cedar for the framework, and the pitch for making the canoe water tight all require time in gathering and preparation. While the canoe is under construction definite perods of waiting are necessary for certain parts of the canoe to dry to form. Ordinarily six persons are required to do the work, four of whom are women. The women sew the birch bark together for the covering and lace the gunwales.

Though other means of transportation long ago superseded the canoe, skillful canoe makers find some demand for good birch bark canoes today.

Birch Bark Containers
(wigwassi makak, s., wigwassi makakon, pl.)

All sorts of containers are made of birch bark by the Ojibwa, both watertight and non-watertight. Troughs for gathering maple sap and other watertight containers with seamless bottom and sides were made by heating a sheet of bark over a small fire or in the steam from boiling water to render it pliable, then bending it in any shape desired. The form into which it was shaped while warm was retained when the bark cooled. The folds are pierced near the ends with an iron awl and fastened together with basswood fiber or skinned spruce roots. The fiber was made flexible by drawing through the mouth several times to dampen it, rolling it between the first finger and the thumb, then heating it over a fire. The watertight receptacles varied in size, the average being about 18 inches in length by 9 inches in width. If the container was very large the edge was reinforced with willow or ash splints laced on with spruce roots. Holes or cracks in the bark were mended with balsam gum or with pitch made from the resin of the bark of black spruce trees. A

Plate 30.   Birch bark basket (mocock) and ricing trays.

basket made of birch bark was sometimes converted into a pail by calking seams with pitch.

To obtain the resin or spruce pitch, cuts were made in the trees and the sap was allowed to gather and harden for a year or more, after which it was whittled off and boiled. In the old days the women made mesh bags of very fine basswood fiber to contain the whittled resin. The bags were then dropped in water and as the pitch came to the top it was skimmed off and placed in birch bark receptacles for future use. The bark and dirt remained in the bag and were destroyed. Supplies of pitch were kept on hand. When needed for use the pitch was heated before applying.

Before metal kettles were available, watertight birch bark containers were used in cooking. This could be done by dropping a series of hot stones into the birch bark container after it had been filled with water. As the first stones cooled other hot ones were added. The Indians say that the watertight birch container could be filled with liquid and set directly over the heat. The bark was thoroughly wet beforehand and the kettle was set over the fire, care being taken that the flames did not touch the bark above the water level.

The "quick pack," used for transporting possessions, consisted of a large sheet of birch bark which was folded up, tied with strips of cedar bark, and provided with a handle of braided cedar bark. In its shape and the purpose for which it was used, it resembled the parfleche bag of rawhide made by the Plains Ojibwa and their western neighbors.

For the non-watertight containers the bark was cut out according to special patterns and sewed up with split roots or basswood fiber. They were used as mococks or makuks for storing maple sugar and wild rice and for gathering cranberries and other fruit, as bowls and serving dishes, and as trays for winnowing wild rice. Very large square or oblong traps (noshkatchinagan, s., noshkatchinaganan, pl.) about 24 inches by 30 inches and 4 and 5 inches deep, firmly sewed and bound around the top with basswood fiber, were provided for the ricing season and kept from year to year.

The mocock is shaped like a truncated pyramid with rounded corners. It varies in size from small trinket boxes to large storage bins which may hold 12 quarts or more. The mococks in which maple sugar is stored hold from 20 to 30 pounds. A high cover of birch bark with slanting sides is sewed over the top of the maple sugar mococks. They are usually made up with the dark surface of the inner bark on the outside, thus providing an effective surface for decoration. A mocock in which berries are to be gathered is provided on one side with a loop of fiber so that it can be hung from a woman's belt as she works. Mococks filled with wild rice were hidden in holes in the earth for future use.

Birch bark boxes made with well fitted covers were usually finished neatly around the top with a rim that was fastened to the container with spruce roots or basswood fiber. Dishes (wigwass onágan, s., wigwass onága-non, pl.), trays, and storage mococks that were for temporary use were not always stiffened and bound at the top.

Decorations Used On Birch Bark

Birch bark containers have been decorated in various ways. The season of the year in which the bark has been gathered has determined in part the type of ornamentation used. Designs have been engraved, scraped, painted, appliqued, and embroidered on the smooth birch bark surfaces. The dark inner surface of the spring peeled bark, which is frequently used as the outside of the container, is often decorated with an engraved design, a sharply pointed piece of bone, preferably the "splint-bone" from the heel of a young doe, being used for the purpose. The light inner color of the bark shows through the lines, contrasting with the dark surface on the upper side.

The scraped patterns, called "self-patterns," are secured by tracing or outlining a design on the dark surface with a sharp stone, bone, or knife, then scraping away the background so that the lighter color underneath is brought out in contrasting shade. Sometimes it was the design that was scraped away, sometimes the background was scraped. When bark is taken from the tree later in the year the dark brown layer adheres to the tree so that etched designs cannot be made on the bark. Designs cut from the winter bark were appliqued with spruce root stitches on baskets made from the summer bark. The birch bark is very light in color when first secured, but it acquires a rich brown color with the passage of the years.

The hour glass, the diagonal border, the zigzag and other geometric designs were engraved on birch bark in all-over design patterns. Curvilinear designs were used on some of the old pieces. Floral designs have always been popular and much used. The floral design is usually used as an isolated unit with no attempt to work in into a design pattern. Skill in the making of engraved and scraped designs on birch bark is still shown in some sections of Minnesota, where they are used on the baskets, pails, and bird houses that are offered to the tourist trade.

In wooded sections where the porcupine is found, porcupine quill embroidery designs have been used to decorate birch bark bowls, boxes, and baskets. The quill designs were usually simple. The Ojibwa south of the Great Lakes did not work out such elaborate quill decorations on their birch bark containers as have the Ottawa and some of the Canadian tribes. All-over quilled designs are seldom found on the Ojibwa birch bark boxes. Isolated

Plate 31.   Birch bark cut-outs.

geometric and floral designs are used on the sides and covers of the boxes. A
cross-stitch done in quills is used to cover the seams on some of the boxes.
(See section on Quill Work, page 120, and frontispiece for illustration).

On the Nett Lake Reservation in Minnesota, and on a number of other
reservations, spruce roots are used both for sewing the seams of the birch
bark boxes and for decorating the rim, lid, and sides. The spruce roots, like
the quills, are sometimes dyed in bright colors. During recent years commercial dyes have been used. The designs used in the spruce root decorations are
much like the isolated unit designs worked out with quills.

Sweet grass has been much used by the Ojibwa as a trimming on their

59

birch bark work. A coil of sweet grass, stitched over and over, frequently serves as a finish around the rim of a container. The use of sweet grass has given rise to no distinctive designs, but has been popular because of the fragrance of the dry grass.

Of late years modern designs, borrowed from many sources, have been used on birch bark.

BASKET MAKING
(Baskets—watabimakak, s., watabimakakon, pl.)

THE art of basketry, though practiced, was not highly developed among the Ojibwa, probably because of the ease with which birch bark could be converted into containers, and of the skill of the Ojibwa in making woven bags that served for carrying and storage purposes. The Ojibwa practiced wicker, plaiting, and coiling techniques using willow branches, basswood bark, black ash splints, cedar root, and sweet grass in their basket making. Most of their baskets were made with handles and covers.

Wickerwork is carried on with a wide or a thick and inflexible vertical warp, and a slender, flexible horizontal weft woven together. The effect on the surface is a series of ridges.

In plaiting, the warp and weft are usually equal in degree of activity and proportions. The elements are woven under-one-over-one so that a checker pattern results or the combinations of elements is varied in such a way that a twilled pattern results.

In coiling, a horizontal warp is sewn over and over with a vertical weft thread of flexible material each stitch interlocking with one immediately beneath it.

Willow Baskets (Wicker)

At an early date wicker baskets were made of willow (Salix sp.). Stripes in contrasting colors could be secured by using willow that was gathered at different seasons of the year, by peeling some of the willow and leaving the remainder green, and by the use of blighted branches. Heavily blighted branches take on a red color, those that are only slighted blighted become brown. Additional colors were secured by the use of native dyes.

In making the wicker baskets, one weft element that is somewhat flexible is passed alternately over and under successive stiff warp elements completely around the basket until a full course is completed. The next weft element follows the same course but goes over those warps under which its

Plate 32.   Basket of willow withes.

predecessor has passed, and vice versa. Since one of the elements is rigid, the effect on the surface is a series of ridges.

The willow baskets were usually round or oval in shape. A covered melon-shaped basket with a bow handle that was arched across the top was one of the types commonly made. Many of the older workers continue to make the willow basket today.

Cedar Root Baskets

Melon shaped wicker baskets were also made of cedar roots. The roots were pulled from the hard ground with considerable care. They were sometimes twenty feet in length. After gathering they were soaked in the lake or pond for several days, scraped and split, then dried, dyed, and soaked again before weaving. The weaving began at the handle and was done on a frame which had been previously constructed and dried.

Baskets of Basswood

A serviceable wicker basket is made of stiff strips from the inner bark of the basswood (Tilia americana L.) following the technique used in making willow baskets described above.

61

Plate 33. Bark bag filled with wild rice.

Baskets of Black Ash

Baskets of wood splints, most commonly black ash (Fraxinus nigra Marsh), are plaited with a simple over-one-under-one weave with two similar elements, in a variety of shapes and serve many useful purposes. Small baskets of split ash are made for use in dice games. The splints are secured by pounding a log with the blunt end of an ax until the sap channels or annual layers are loosened and can be peeled off in thin layers. These are then cut into thin splints, stained or dyed, and woven over and under one another in vertical, horizontal, or diagonal positions. As the splints vary in width and are dyed in different colors much variety is secured in the decorative effects. The splints in some of the old baskets are a rich brown in color.

The technique followed in the black ash baskets is a plaiting or checker work like that of the common market basket. Plain plaiting is made by passing the elements over one and under one. The warp and weft are usually indistinguishable, being of the same size and shape and equally active. Plaiting differs from wicker work in that the latter has distinct warps and wefts.

A diagonal or twilled plaiting is secured by passing the splints over and under each other in other combinations, such as over two and under two, over one under two, or over one under three, or over three and under three, or in any combination or variation of these. In passing one splint over the others the passage is alternated row after row so that a variety of angular, diamond, and diagonal patterns results. Sometimes the combinations change as the work progresses.

About 1860 around the Great Lakes a curl was introduced in the splint basket work. This new technique known as "curled" work or "porcupine" work continues in use to a limited extent today. In the curled work a thin horizontal splint is carried over the vertical splints and twisted or curled at regular intervals to produce a series of outstanding points or "curls" that provide an effective relief decoration on the surface of the basket. The term "porcupine work" is descriptive of the technique and has nothing to do with porcupine quills.

All this is very similar to the Seneca splint basketry thoroughly described in the pamphlet of that title by Marjorie Lismer. (See listing on page 4.)

Baskets of Sweet Grass
(wicko-mashkossiw, s., wicko-mashkossiwan, pl.)

Sweet grass [Hierochloë odorata (L.) Beauv. (Torresia odorata Hitchc.)], in some places known as Seneca grass, vanilla grass, and holy grass, is a native of the northern section of North America. It is a semi-erect grass that seldom reaches a height of over 2½ feet and usually grows among shrubs and other grasses. It is harvested before it ripens from the middle of June until the time when it begins to dry in September. Though it is usually gathered casually, sometimes a whole family may devote a day or two to gathering it. It is dried in the shade so that it will hold its color longer.

Sweet grass has but little odor when growing or when first gathered, but as it dries the color fades and, due to an essential oil, a delicate fragrance similar to vanilla is given off. Since primitive times it has been widely used by the Indians as perfume and incense in ceremonial observances and in the making of baskets. The Ojibwa were probably making coiled baskets with sweet grass before the coming of the Whites. Sweet grass is also used on splint and bark baskets to provide borders, handles, fastenings, decorative designs and other trimmings and to impart a pleasant fragrance.

In making the coiled sweet grass basket the grass is gathered into a coil about one-fourth inch in diameter, a knot is made in the end of the coil, and around it the coil is wrapped and secured by sewing from the bottom to the rim of the basket. In the old days a native fiber was used as thread, and a basket maker's bone awl took the place of a needle. The awl was used to

Plate 34. Coiled sweet-grass basket.

make the holes through which the fiber was passed. The primitive awl, which was an aboriginal implement, had a point that was slightly rounded so that it could find its way between the stitches of the coil beneath and not pierce the grasses. The thread is passed around the free portion of the coil, back into the previous coil which has already been attached, and under the stitch that was taken in the last round so that the stitches of one round interlock with those of the previous round. It is pulled tight to bind the last round firmly to the previous coil. The stitches are rather far apart. The coils vary in thickness according to the size of the basket to be made.

The coiled basket is often built up on a base of birch bark, the bark being used as the center with the coils of sweet grass sewed around it. Sometimes the basket is provided with a birch bark lid on which there is an incised or quilled design. Handles are seldom added to the baskets.

Round and oval bowls, flat mats, shallow dishes and trays, trinket baskets, and numerous small articles were made of coiled sweet grass. Sweet grass was used both as a finish and a decoration for baskets of other materials, to which it imparted a pleasant fragrance.

WOVEN YARN BANDS AND SASHES
(miskogad, s., miskogadog, pl.)

B RAIDING, netting or looping, and weaving were among the arts early practiced by the American Indians. In the old days they braided, netted, or wove bands, pack straps, garters, and sashes of buffalo wool, working out designs with the lighter and darker shades of undyed wool and with wools colored with native dyes. Explorers of the seventeenth century refer to the brightly colored belts and bands of buffalo wool worn by the Woodland Indians (Marquette, 1673).

The garters and broad sashes formed a decorative part of the costume of both the men and the women. Old pictures dated 1743 and 1792 show men with woven garters tied around the knees and sashes wrapped around the head like a turban, tied around the buckskin jacket to keep it closed, or thrown across one shoulder like a soldier's belt. There is little evidence of the use of the garters and sash in the woman's costume except to support the leggings and skirt.

These yarn bands and sashes of the Woodland Indians show a marked similarity to the garters and sashes (ceintures fléchées) woven in Canada for the voyageurs of the North West Company in the early part of the eighteenth century and later for the bourgeois of the Hudson Bay Company. By the early part of the eighteenth century the sash had become increasingly popular both in Canada and among the Indians of the northeastern woodlands of the United States and its vogue seems to have continued well up toward the end of the century.

In Bulgaria, Norway, and Lapland woven yarn garters much like those of the Woodland Indians have formed a part of the native costumes. A similar type of weaving has apparently been practiced by primitive people in various parts of the world. Whether finger weaving is native to the Indians or had been introduced among them by the women of other countries is a question that gives rise to much speculation. That the Indians developed distinctive designs and carried the art to a high degree of perfection cannot be questioned.

Before 1890 mechanically woven sashes manufactured in England were put on the market by Hudson Bay Company and sold at a much lower price ($1.00 to $3.25) than were the hand-woven sashes that often brought from $15.00 to $25.00. Today the old hand-made sashes usually bring a very high price.

In the last decade of the seventeenth century after the introduction of blankets and other mechanically woven textiles the Indian women secured yarn for the sashes by ravelling materials which they secured from the traders. The yarn thus secured was respun and redyed with native dyes. Red was obtained from blankets and uniforms. In the early part of the nineteenth century commercial yarns in crimson and other colors became available through the North West Company and apparently a new interest arose in the making of the handwoven bands and sashes which led to the development of new techniques and new designs. The skill with which the Indian women handled the imported yarns was undoubtedly an outgrowth of their previous mastery of the old Indian weaving techniques practiced with buffalo wool and the native vegetables dyes.

The term "Woodland sashes" is used in the text, but sashes woven by the old Indian weave were worn by some of the Plains Indians as well as by the Indians of the eastern woodlands. Whether these were made by the women of the tribe or obtained by trade from some of the Woodland Indians has not been determined. A similar finger weave was used in the production of similar articles of weaving apparel by the Pueblo Indians. (See "Pueblo Crafts" by Ruth Underhill, Indian Handcraft Series.)

McKenney and Hall in "Indian Tribes in North America" published in 1827 show woven sashes worn by a Cree and a Seminole. In pictures painted by Catlin between 1840 and 1850 a yarn sash and garters are shown on a Seminole Indian and sashes are pictured on the Sauk, Iowa, Muskogee and Choctaw Indians as well as on many Woodland Indians.

Though the Ojibwa practiced the art of braiding or weaving sashes to a more limited extent than did their neighbors, the Winnebago and the Menomini, even today they have not entirely forgotten the old Indian techniques and attempts to revive them during recent years have met with gratifying results. Sashes can be secured on order from some of the Ojibwa women as well as from women of other tribes where a similar revival has taken place.

The following paragraphs describe braiding, netting, and weaving as practiced by the Woodland Indians.

Braiding

In braiding, three or more lengthwise or warp strands are crossed diagonally and lengthwise in such a way that each of them lies alternately over and under one or several of the others thus making a texture with the use of warp threads only. Bands, belts, and fringes for bags and sashes were braided. Today the Indian women braid bands with many strands of colored rags making rugs of modern types.

Netting

When netting or looping was to be done, strands of the desired length

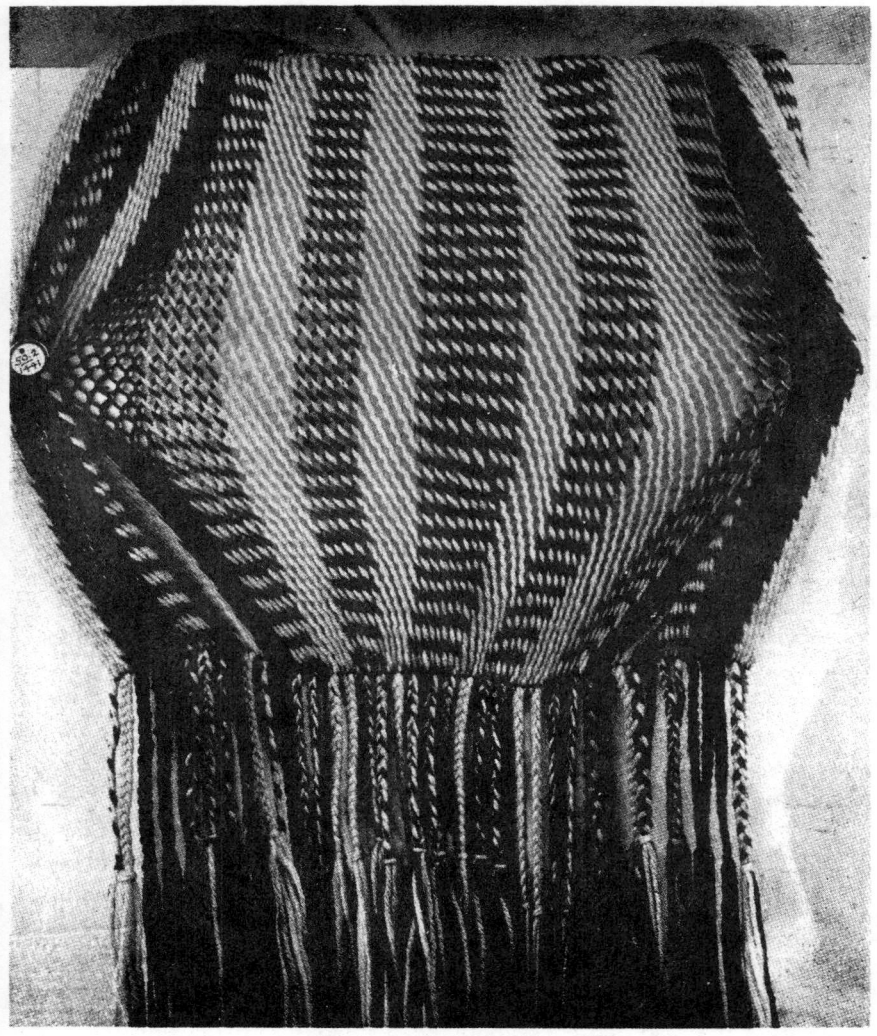

Plate 35.　Netted sash (modern).

were firmly anchored at one end so that all would run lengthwise. Then each strand in turn was carried diagonally across the strand on either side and looped or knotted with it to form meshes of uniform size, producing an open, elastic fabric. In the loose looping which the Minnesota women used in making the netted or looped yarn sash the loops are formed by making only half twists. In the regular netting such as the men used in making fish nets each strand was knotted with the neighboring strands.

The Netted or Looped Sash

Netted sashes are about nine inches wide and two yards or more in length. The designs in the netted sashes are in straight line stripes. On some sashes the stripes are crossed at right angles by a short bar or arm that extends beyond the stripe on each side. The cross bar is secured by alternating the colors when the sash is set up. The netted sashes do not show so great a variety in design as do the woven sashes.

In making the netted sash the yarn is wound off in the desired length across two stakes. When a sufficient amount had been wound off, the stakes are loosened and the strands of yarn are drawn together into a space the width of the sash to be made. A thread is then passed horizontally in and out between the strands separating the colors. This is made firm by slipping a split stick over the yarn and attaching it at each end, to hold the threads in position for netting.

The yarn strands are cut through near one of the stakes and the long skein is attached with a string or strip of cloth to a stake at each end to support it and give it the proper tension.

The worker seats herself beside the skein to begin the work of netting. To do the netting the strands are separated into two levels according to colors. The left hand is used to separate the threads and to hold them apart. They may be tied temporarily with a bit of yarn to prevent their being intermingled.

The right fore-finger is then used as a hook to catch up one of the lower threads and bring it against the neighboring upper thread. The right thumb and fore-finger are used to twist the threads together.

The left hand and its threads are held below the right hand. As the thread is raised and twisted it is moved to the right, the thread around which it has been twisted being moved to the left and allowed to fall into the lower bunch of threads, at the left edge. The twist is always made from left to right and the netting proceeds from left to right of the worker. All the threads to the left pass under and those to the right pass over. The work proceeds across the width of the sash and back again. Each thread is twisted with the same two threads alternately throughout the length of the sash, first the one on the left and then the one on the right. Sometimes beads are threaded on the yarn and as the netting proceeds the beads help form a pattern. When the netting is completed the split stick and the yarn stitches are removed and the ends are finished with a fringe in the same way as on the woven sashes.

Weaving

Technically, weaving can be described as a process by which two sets of strings, yarns, or strands of either spun or twisted materials are so interlaced as to form a continuous web. One system of th eads or strands, called woof or weft, passes alternately under and over another system (or group) of threads called warp, web, or chain. Weaving is done both by hand and on a loom. In loom weaving the essential operations are the raising of certain threads of the warp and the depression of others to form a shed for the passage of the weft strand which is then beaten down by means of a lathe or batten. The raising of the threads can be done with the fingers but is usually accomplished by the use of a heddle or loom, which is a convenience, though not necessary.

The Ojibwa weaving was carried on both with and without a loom. Different techniques were used in weaving mats, bags, and sashes. Most of these techniques resemble those that have been practiced by other primitive people. For many years native vegetable fibers and the wool of the buffalo provided the material for weaving. Commercial threads and yarns have long been used by the Ojibwa in their weaving.

Though there are few prehistoric pieces of woven materials remaining, imprints of weaving can be studied on old pottery shards where the textile impressions were used to decorate the surface of the vessels. That any of this early weaving or pottery was the work of the ancestors of the present Ojibwa has not been authentically determined. The later Ojibwa have woven sashes, mats, and bags in various styles and techniques that display native skill and a feeling for design and color that make the work of special interest. The technique used in making the Woodland sashes is today known among the Indians as "old Indian weave." Twined weaving techniques were used in making storage bags and in some of the rush mats. Other mats were made with a simple over-and-under weave, basswood fiber being used as weft. In making cedar bark bags and mats a checker or twilled design was secured by using warp and weft of the same material and equal in width, with the over-and-under or plaited weave. Cat-tail mats were sewed together with a basswood fiber.

Old Indian Weave or Finger Weaving

The old Indian weave used by the Woodland tribes in making garters, bands, and sashes differs from mechanical weaving in that there is no separate set of weft threads and no loom is necessary nor is a heddle or shuttle used, the entire process is carried on with the fingers. There is only one set of threads, the lengthwise or warp threads which are interlaced with one another instead of with an additional set of threads. Thus the one set of threads serves as both warp and weft. The threads hang loose so that the process is sometimes designated as loose warp weaving. The work is carried on•downward. When the weaving begins, each warp thread in turn becomes a weft

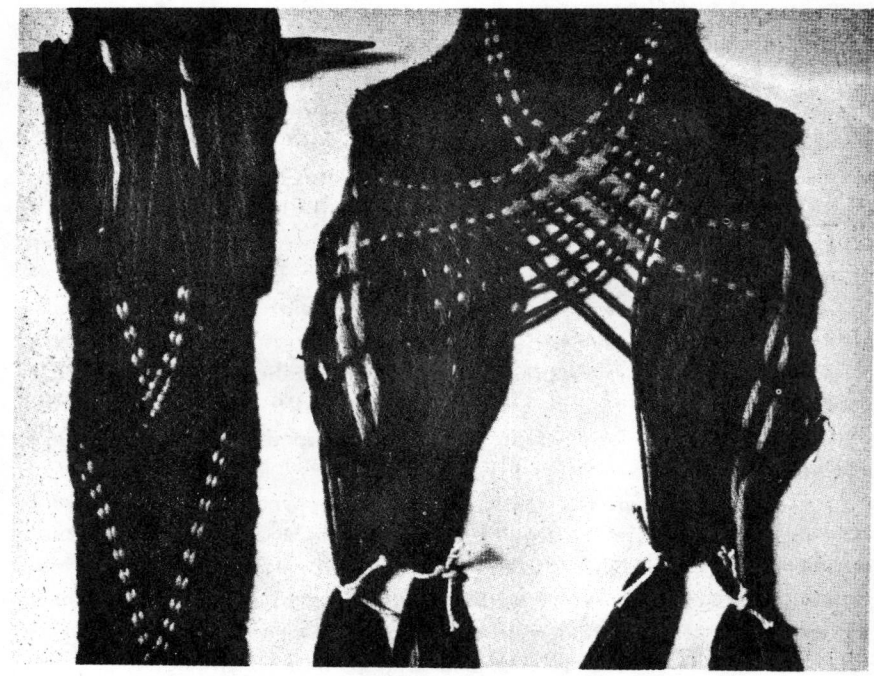

Plate 36.   Woodland sash, old Indian finger weave.

thread and is drawn by the fingers, without a shuttle, through a shed which is formed by separating the alternate warp threads and is kept open by the fingers. After the thread which is serving as a weft thread has passed through, the shed is allowed to close and the fingers are used to press or beat it up. The end of the acting weft thread is dropped after it has passed through the shed and it once more becomes a warp thread. A new shed is then opened up by the fingers for the next acting weft thread. Each warp thread may serve as a weft thread many times during the weaving of a sash.

Types of Articles Woven

Among the Woodland Indians narrow bands about 1½ inches to 2 inches wide and 24 inches long were woven with 20 or more threads for use as garters to support the leggings or as arm bands. Broader bands were woven or netted to be worn as sashes. The number of strands used determined the width of the band or sash. In the 4 inch sash 140 threads were used. The sashes were from 4 to 12 inches wide and from 3 to 15 feet long. They were usually finished at each end with a fringe 12 or more inches in length. Occasionally a fringe was as long as a yard and three quarters. The narrow bands were also finished with a fringe several inches in length. The long fringes were usually braided or twisted. The end was knotted and often finished with a tuft of wool. The fringe served not only as a decoration, but also to tie the band or sash in place when worn.

The Woodland sash was usually woven with yarns in three or more colors, deep red predominating. With it were combined two shades of blue, sage green, old gold, and white. Well twisted commercial yarns in 2 ply or 3 ply were dyed with native dyes to secure these colors. Variations in the weave and in the arrangement of the colors in relation to one another brought out the patterns characteristic of these old sashes. Large white beads were sometimes worked in with the yarn as the weaving progressed, producing geometric patterns.

The designs included stripes, triangles, hexagons, diamonds or slanting lozenges, saw-tooth designs, zigzag or lightning, the hour glass, and V and W shaped designs. The two latter both appear in the sturgeon flesh pattern, popular with the Minnesota Ojibwa. The arrow design, seen in many old sashes, was not used to a great extent by the Ojibwa. In some of the sashes an open work weave added to the beauty of the design.

Method of Weaving a Woodland Sash

When a sash was to be woven by the old Indian technique, a well twisted yarn that had been spun in two or three strands was dyed with native dyes in the color desired. The sash was then woven from end to end or from mid-way of the whole length of the strands, first toward one end then toward the other end. In the weaving of the sash from one end, the following steps were taken:

Step I.   The variously colored yarns were wound off in a skein of the length and the number of strands desired for the sash. In estimating the length of the yarn strands, it was necessary to remember that they were to form both the warp and the weft and, therefore, they would run diagonally of the sash. To this estimate, the length of the fringe at both ends had to be added.

The required length of yarn was secured by driving two sticks into the ground at a distance from one another that would provide strands of the desired length as the yarn was wound around the tops of the sticks. The yarn was carried around the sticks as many times as the number of strands needed. In order to wind the yarn about the sticks, one end was first fastened to one of the sticks, then the yarn was carried across to the other stick and back, being wound around the two sticks until as many strands of that color had been secured as desired. The end of a strand of another color was then knotted to the end of the strand of the first color and the second color was carried around the tops of the sticks as many times as there were strands desired for the pattern that was to be worked out. Other colors were added in the same manner.

Step II. When a sufficient number of strands of all the desired colors had been wound off, the skein was removed from the sticks and cut through at one end.

Step III. The length of the fringe was measured off at one end, and a piece of yarn, string, or cotton cloth was tied twice around the set of strands at the point where the fringe was to end and the weaving to begin. Then the strands were looped over a split stick 6 or 8 inches long so that they were spread out. The other end of the skein of yarn was tied with twine or cloth to hold the strands together. The cotton string at one end was then attached to a stake driven into the ground, and the other end was attached to the waist of the worker to hold the skein taut and steady. It was necessary for the worker to sit down to carry on the further steps in weaving the sash.

Step IV. The strands were then arranged according to color in the order desired for the pattern. If a V or lightning pattern was desired and 50 strands of woolen yarn were used, the following arrangement of colors was necessary—13 red, 1 yellow, 1 red, 1 yellow, 3 brown, 2 red, 4 green, 4 green, 2 red, 3 brown, 1 yellow, 1 red, 1 yellow, 13 red. To arrange the strands in order, two lengthwise strands were picked up at one time and enclosed in two crosswise yarn strands, one crosswise strand was carried under them, another crosswise strand over the same two, and the two crosswise strands were given a half turn before the next two vertical strands were picked up. At the end the crosswise strands were doubled back to form a loop around the first two vertical strands. The two crosswise strands were then tied together. They were removed when the sash was completed or were left with the ends hanging to form a part of the fringe.

Step V. The yarn was then divided in the center, half on the left side and half on the right side. Beginning left to right the index finger of the left hand was used as a heddle to pick up every other strand and to drop the alternate strands on the left side thus forming a shed that extended to the center with half the strands.

Step VI. The last strand (X) on the left side, which was in the upper half of the left shed, and the first strand (Y) on the right side, which was in the lower half of the right shed, were then crossed in the center. (X) was picked up and carried to the left through the shed which had been formed by picking up every other strand. The (X) strand thus became the weft. When

Step No. I   Winding off the yarn

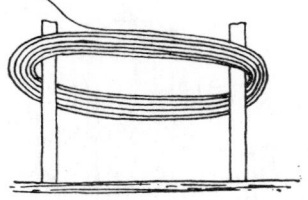

Step No. II   Cutting the strands of yarn

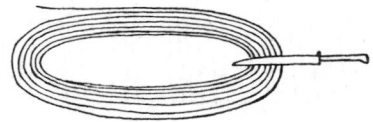

Step No III   Tying the skein of yarn

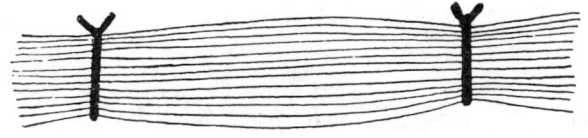

Step No. IV   Arranging the strands

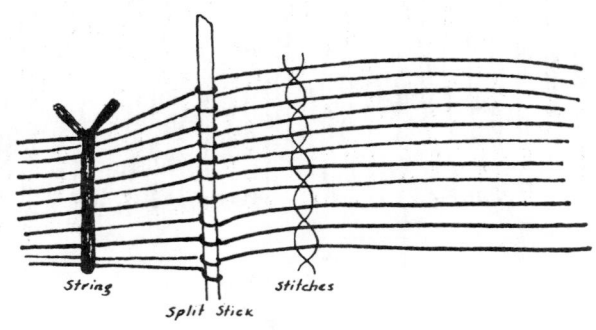

String   Split Stick   Stitches

Plate 37.   Weaving a woodland sash Steps I-IV.

Step No. V   Forming the shed

Center
Y ↓ x

Step No. VI Carrying the first strand through the shed

Center
Y ↓ x

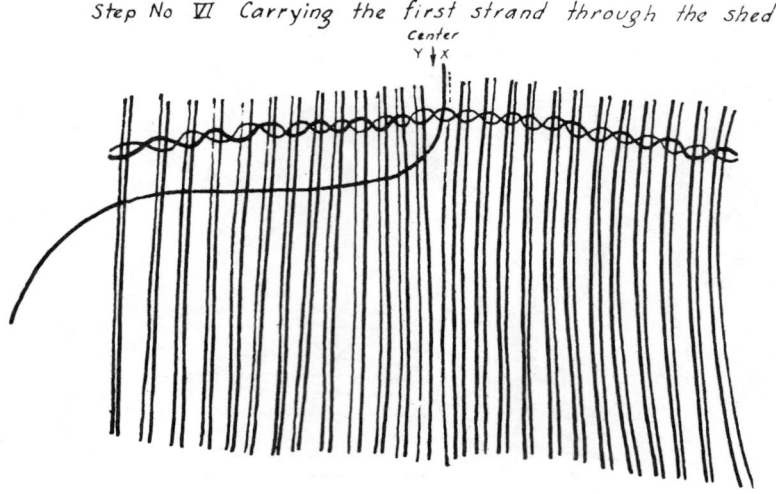

Plate 38.   Weaving a woodland sash Steps V and VI.

the thread (X) reached the edge of the sash, it was dropped and again became a warp strand.

With the index finger of the left hand a new shed was made by alternately picking up the strands on the lower half of the shed and dropping those on the upper half of the shed, so that the thread (X) that had been carried through the shed to the left was completely woven in.

Step VII. All this time the right side of the sash had been idle. Now the work was done with the right side only, and the portion that had been the left side was idle. The belt was turned over so that the right half of the belt now became the left half and the process that had been carried on as Step VI was repeated with what had been the right half of the belt, using (Y) as the weft strand.

Step VIII. As each strand was carried to the left and dropped at the side, the sash was turned over and the center strands were crossed and were woven in as X and Y had been. This process was continued until the sash was of the required length. When the weaving of the sash was finished the split stick and usually the crosswise yarn stitches at the end were removed and the sash was finished with a fringe which was twisted or braided. The braided fringes were both flat and round.

Methods of Making Fringe

To make the twisted fringe, the following steps were taken:

1. Two strands or more of the fringe were rolled between the palms of the hands or on the thigh down toward the knee.

2. Two more strands of the fringe were rolled on the thigh down toward the knee.

3. The ends of the two pieces of fringe were then held together and the two sets of strands were rolled in opposite directions from the first rolling or twisting.

4. A knot was made at the end to hold the twisted fringe securely.
To make the flat braided fringe.

When the flat fringe was to be braided, three groups of three strands each were picked up at a time at the point where the weaving stopped, and the fringe was made up into tight braids. Knots were made at the ends of each of the braids.

To make the round braided fringe (See plate 39):

Four strands were used to make the round braided fringe. Two strands were of one color, two of another—for example. two red and two green

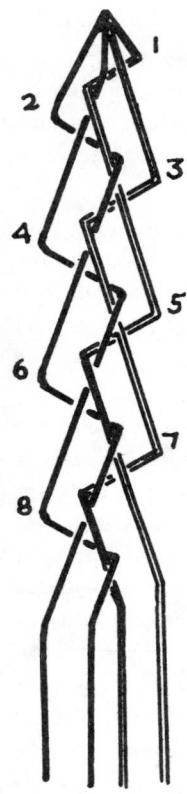

Plate 39. Making round braided fringe.

strands. The work was arranged so that the two dark strands shown by the solid line were at the left, the two light strands shown by the double line, at the right of the diagram.

The top or outside light (double line 1) strand was carried from right to left behind two strands and brought forward between the two dark (solid) strands, then carried to the right across the center dark strand.

Next, the top or outside dark (solid line 2) strand was carried behind two strands from left to right and brought forward between the two light strands and carried across the center light strand to the left.

Strands may then be tightened up in pairs to show their general relative positions. The outside strand (whether it was on the right or the left side) which was the highest in the braid, was always the one which was carried behind two strands and back over one strand.

While the weaving of the round fringe was in process the braid was not allowed to turn around, but was kept with the same side toward the worker. After each operation the strands were straightened out in parallel pairs to show how the work was progressing. The braid was usually knotted at the end and often finished with a fine fringe or tassel.

WOVEN BAGS
(mashkimod, s., mashkimodan, pl.)

F LAT, rectangular storage or carrying bags woven of native materials are among the most interesting of the old Ojibwa craft articles, and are much prized by the older members of the tribe. The art of twined weaving used in the making of the bags was practiced in common by many of the tribes with whom the Ojibwa were associated around the Great Lakes and in the Mississippi Valley. The making of woven bags was practiced not only by the Ojibwa, but also by the Menomini, Potawatomi, Sauk, Fox, Miami, and Kickapoo of the Algonquin stock, and the Winnebago, Iowa, Osage, and Santee or Eastern Sioux.

The bags were made by a process known as "loose warp" weaving, as all the warp was left hanging loosely by one end from a horizontal support, and the fabric was built from the top, down. In the weaving, two series of threads were woven at right angles. The weft threads were arranged in pairs to cross the warp threads. One weft thread was carried over a warp thread or a pair of warp threads. The other weft thread passed behind the warp thread or the pair of warp threads. At each intersection the two weft threads were twisted half way around each other enclosing the warp thread. The weft threads were introduced at intervals of varying width, usually from one quarter to three quarters of an inch apart. The warps were sometimes crowded together. At other times the warps were spaced some distance apart so that an open work weave was produced. A zigzag weave was also common in the old bags. In the zigzag or twilled weave the weft threads were carried over paired warp threads which were separated and brought together alternately in the successive rows of weaving.

The construction of the bags demanded a peculiar skill. The techniques necessarily varied with the materials used and with the different workers. A well-made bag would last a hundred years or more.

Bags of Nettle Weed Fiber

One of the oldest of the woven bags was that made of the fiber of the false nettle usually combined with buffalo or moose hair or wool, spun with the fingers into a thread or cord. The nature of the nettle stalk fibers and their preparation for use have been described in the section dealing with native cord and twine.

In the early days buffalo roamed the woodland regions as far north as the Great Lakes. After 1800 when the herds east of the Mississippi had disappeared the Ojibwa were probably able to secure buffalo hides through trade with the Winnebago, Sauk, Fox, Potawatomi, Sioux, and other plains Indians.

The buffalo has two types of hair, a coarse protective hair and a fine wool which is shed in the spring. The coarse hair is stiff and varies in length from 4 to 11 inches. That from the head, neck, and shoulders is longest. The wool which covers the body, is short, fine, and smooth, as soft to the touch as velvet. It is dun, rust, or light reddish brown in color. The coarse hair is a dark brown, almost black.

The moose was plentiful in the northern regions and is still to be found in northern Minnesota where it has been protected in the game preserves. A "mane" or "bell" made up of long hairs hangs from the throat of the moose. In the bull-moose these hairs are 5 or 6 inches in length and become very coarse and stiff in winter. The hairs are a brownish or purplish gray growing light toward the roots so that they are nearly white at the root end. The color of the moose hair varies with the background and the season. White hairs are most abundant on the winter killed moose. The darkest hair is found on the moose in the pine forests.

A very soft, light brown wool grows thickly near the roots of the hair and all over the body of the moose, though there is very little of it in some places. Both the hair and wool of the moose were probably made use of by the Ojibwa at one time.

In the early nettle fiber bags used for ceremonial purposes, patterns were worked out by a combination of the light nettle fiber with the wool of the moose or the darker buffalo wool. Later wool ravelings from blankets and old clothing were redyed and respun to be used in developing the designs. In weaving, a crowding of the weft strands brought the warp strands to the front and left the other color inside. The color of the figures on the outside, therefore, differed from the color of those on the inside. The making of the nettle fiber bags is no longer practiced. Many old bags have been preserved in museum collections.

Bags of Basswood Bark Fiber

The early bags were also made of roots, rushes, and fibers from the barks of the cedar, slippery elm, and the linden or basswood tree. Basswood fiber long continued in use as weft in making yarn bags.

In the preparation of fiber from basswood bark, it was necessary to soak or boil it. If it was boiled in a metal kettle the basswood took on a tannish red that contributed to the beauty of the bags.

To make bags of basswood fiber, strips of untwisted fiber about one-eighth of an inch or more in width which were to serve as warp were hung over

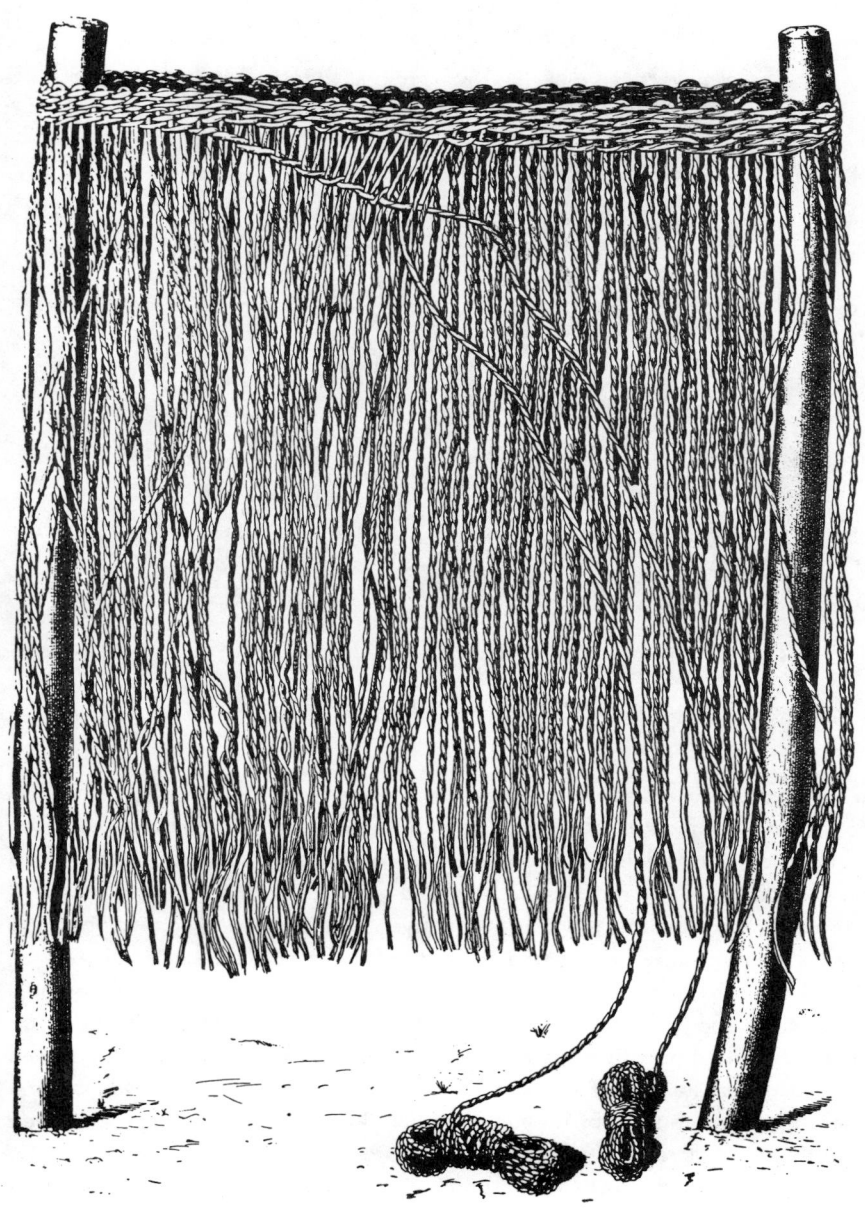

Plate 40.   Bag being twined on the simple two-stick loom.

Plate 41. Unfinished basswood bark bag.

a suspended rod so that they were equally long on both sides of the rod. Before being put on the rod a pair of weft threads of twisted basswood fiber running at right angles to the warp was carried across the untwisted warp threads on top of the rod. One weft passed behind, and the other in front of a warp or group of warps, then they were given a half turn and carried on to the next warp or group of warps and given a half twist between each, all the way across the rod. Another pair of wefts was then carried across the warps at a distance of about one inch below the rod, over and under each warp or group of warps, with a half turn between each, in the same way that they had been carried across the rod. The second pair of wefts passes all the way around the warps on both sides of the rod. Additional rows of weft threads are woven into the warp at regular intervals. The portion of the bag that rested on the rod formed the bottom of the finished bag so that no bottom seam was necessary nor were any side seams necessary, since the weft threads were carried continuously around the warp on both sides of the bag.

Open work weaves were secured in the basswood bags (a) by pairing the warps and working out vertical zigzag patterns and (b) by crossing the warps at a sharp angle to secure a lattice effect with hexagonal interstices as shown in the drawings.

The ends of the warp strips as they hung from the rod were usually left long enough so that they could be brought together for a finish at the top when the bag was removed from the rod. Groups of from 3 to 5 warp strands were twisted into a heavier strand for a short distance, then gathered into a continuous coil or a tight braid that was carried around the top to provide a firm finish to the bag. On other bags a strip of basswood two or more inches deep, woven in the same technique as that used in the body of the bag, was sewed firmly across the top of the bag giving it added strength.

The design on the basswood bag is the same on both sides. It is usually a vertical stripe or panel secured by the arrangement of the colors used in the warp.

Woven Yarn Bags

The first yarn bags were probably made of buffalo hair, which the writings of the early travelers lead us to think the Indians had learned to spin and weave with skill before they came into contact with the Europeans. When commercial yarns and woolen goods were brought into this country during the seventeenth century, the Indians began to substitute them for their native products, and bags were woven of commercial yarn. In their eagerness to secure materials for bags, the Ojibwa laboriously frayed out woolen blankets and cast-off trade clothing, respun the wool, and redyed it so that they could use it as weft thread in weaving bags. Nettle fiber and basswood bark continued to be used as the warp. Native dyes were used to color the commercial yarns when they first came into use. Later colored commercial twine and yarns and commercial dyes were introduced and today they have almost wholly supplanted the native materials.

During recent years the making of yarn bags has been carried on for commercial purposes by the Lac du Flambeau Indians in Wisconsin where bags have been made in many of the homes. The art of making yarn bags has also been preserved at Odanah and among the Lac Courte Oreilles in Wisconsin and among the Cass Lake Indians in Minnesota where the younger women have enjoyed practicing the technique.

When a bag was to be made of yarn, two strong but springy smooth rods about 36 inches long and one half inch in diameter were secured firmly in a log or in the ground at a distance slightly wider than the width of the proposed bag so that the spring of the wood would keep the work in place

Plate 42.   Woven bag of raveled blanket yarn.

while the weaving was being done. A loop of heavy cord to which the necessary number of warps of the desired length were previously attached was then stretched around the top of the rods. Care was taken to space the warp threads evenly as they were attached to the cord. The warps were left to hang unattached at the bottom, no tension being applied in the weaving. The weaver began her work just below the cord at what was to be eventually the bottom of the bag, and worked downward. She twined a pair of variously colored wefts around each warp, one at a time, or around two if the warp thread was very thin, all the way around the bag, placing each round close below the previous one. The manipulation of the cords or strings required great skill. Several varieties of twining were used. When the warp threads had been covered for almost their entire length, and the bag was the required size, it was removed from the supporting rods and the edge which was uppermost was sewed together in a seam to form the bottom of the bag. The loose

ends of the warp were folded over and wrapped to form a corded edge at the top of the bag. Below the cord a space of open work was left, through which a cord was laced in and out to close the bag when it was filled. No handles were provided. The bags were usually twenty inches by twenty inches. Larger yarn bags were sometimes made. Very small bags were made to be carried in the medicine bundle.

Designs Used On Woven Bags

Strips, bands, and small geometric patterns were used on many of the woven bags. Conventionalized figures of animals that had part in the mythology of the tribe are found on the old nettle fiber bags. These figures include the thunder bird, underground panther, deer, butterfly, and the tracks of the otter.

Plate 44. An unfinished yarn bag (modern cotton carpetwarp).

The thunder bird occurs in many of the old myths of Indian tribes throughout Canada and the northern United States. It was thought of as a great bird that dwelt on a high mountain or rocky elevation difficult of access. The dark cloud was the shadow, the flapping of its wings made the sound of thunder, its flashing eyes, rapidly opening and closing, sent forth the lightning. It was the duty of the thunder bird to bring hail and rain to the earth and to guard man.

Prehistoric representations of the thunder bird are found engraved or carved on stone or pottery. At a later period representations of the thunder bird were drawn on birch bark, painted on skins, woven on the bags of nettle fiber and buffalo hair, and worked out in porcupine quill and bead designs by the Ojibwa and their neighbors.

Belief in an underground panther, a mythical giant with buffalo horns and a long curling tail drawn under his feet, was held by the Ojibwa, Menomini, and Winnebago tribes. Only medicine men, after long periods of

Plate 45.   Modern woven yarn bag.

fasting, had seen such an animal. The Ojibwa women worked out representations of the underground panther on bags of nettle fiber and buffalo hair.

The old bags of basswood and others of this type have a central panel with vertical side stripes. These are the same on the two sides of the bag. The designs on the two sides of the nettle fiber and yarn bags often differ.

Designs on the yarn bags usually show three major broad horizontal bands with two minor narrow bands between them. The diamond, the hour glass, the zigzag, the elongated hexagon, and various combinations of angles were used within the broad band.

Pattern motifs on the old bags were in a large measure determined by the materials and techniques used. Many of the patterns were used by several different tribes, but there is some indication that each tribe gave the designs individual treatment. There was probably an exchange of bags between tribes, and the bags found by a collector in one tribe may have been made by the women of a neighboring tribe. In the old days bag making may have given rise to a wholesome rivalry between the women of the different tribes, leading to an unconscious imitation of patterns.

Cedar Bark Bags, Plaited

Bags of various shapes were woven of untwisted cedar bark fibers. Vertical, diagonal, checkered, and twilled weaving or plaiting were used. There was no distinction between the warp and weft in the plaiting.

A cedar bark bag woven without a seam across the bottom continues to be used as one of the containers for storing wild rice, one of the most valuable of the native foods. The bag is woven with a vertical or a diagonal weave. The strips of fibers are hung across a single stick which is suspended at the ends so that the weaver can work on both sides.

The weaving is carried on downward from the stick and shaped into a square or oblong bag. When the bag is finished the stick is removed and the corners are folded under and sewed down. As in the other woven bags an open work space is left just below the upper edge, and through this the bag is laced together with basswood fiber after it has been filled with the wild rice. The rice is covered at the top with a layer of hay.

Plate 47.   Unfinished cedar bark rice bag.

Tamarack Bags [Larix laricina (Du Roi) Koch]

To make bags of tamarack roots (watáb, s., watában, pl.), it was necessary to first split and boil the roots of the tamarack so that they were sufficiently pliable to be woven. The weaving was carried on in the same way that the bark bags were woven. The tamarack bags were used for storing medicinal herbs and roots, and for wild rice.

WOVEN MATS
(anákan, s., anákanan, pl.)

A MONG the Ojibwa the women spent the summer in making lodge coverings (apákwei, s., apákweiag, pl.) and mats (anákan, s., anákanan, pl.) and in picking and drying berries. Much of the mat making fell to the older women who could no longer do the heavy work around the lodge. The gathering of bulrushes ⟨Scirpus validus Vahl⟩ and cattails ⟨Typha latifolia L⟩ for their mats was one of the activities of special interest to the women. The rushes (anákanashk, s., anákanashkon, pl.) were gathered from canoes in late June and July after they were full grown. Before beginning the work of weaving mats, it was necessary to gather, bleach, dry, and dye the rushes, to make fiber cord and bone needles, and to erect a simple frame upon

Plate 48.   Weaving rush mats.
a.   After reeds have been interlaced the basswood bark is woven across the mat.
b.   A finished mat and one in its first stages.

Plate 49. An unfinished rush mat on frame.

which to construct the mat. The weaving frame consisted of a horizonta pole supported by two vertical poles. It was usually set up out of doors under a temporary shelter of leaves or other shade. A cool dark shed was used to hold the supply of birch bark, rushes ⟨Scirpus validus Vahl⟩, and strips of basswood bark ⟨Tilian americana L.⟩. Sometimes a special building in which to carry on the work was constructed of jack-pine bark which kept the interior cool and somewhat damp. The door was toward the north so that the sun could not shine in, and it was closed when not in use in order to keep the supplies in good condition.

Rush Mats

When a bulrush mat was to be made, a two-ply basswood cord (ana-kaneiab, s., anakaneiabin, pl.) was measured off to equal the length of the proposed mat, and the ends of the necessary number of rushes were turned down and twisted onto the cord, one by one, to make a firm edge. Then the cord, with the rushes attached, was fastened at intervals to the horizontal pole supported by the two vertical poles which constituted the weaving frame. The horizontal pole was placed at a height above the ground somewhat greater than the width of the proposed mat so that the rushes hung loose above the ground. The width of the mat was determined by the length of the rushes. Mats were usually from 36 to 45 inches wide and from 2 to 3 yards long. They could be as long as desired.

The hanging rushes formed the warp of the mat. Basswood twine was used for the weft. The weaving progressed downward. No shuttle was used. The weaver carried the ball of twine in one hand and separated the rushes with the other so that the twine could pass between them. Sometimes two wefts were used, one on either side of the warp. The wefts were passed around each warp and twined together, thus each weft passed from the front to the back of the mat and vice versa.

It was important that the rushes be kept damp while the work progressed. This necessitated working in the early morning when the atmosphere was filled with moisture and there could be no danger of the sun drying out the rushes. Considerable time was consumed in making the mat. Occasionally on a rainy day several women would work together on a mat, completing it in a short time. When the mat was finished, the lower end was "bound off" by turning up the ends of the rushes and fastening them as they had been fastened to the cord at the upper end.

Simple designs were secured by the use of dyed rushes, woven in narrow stripes, usually so grouped as to form broader stripes at intervals across the mat. Colored rushes were sometimes worked in diagonally to form a pattern in lattice work or with elongated diamond shaped figures. A diagonal plaid was woven by carrying one half the rushes diagonally to the left, the other half to the right. Designs were also secured by the combination of different techniques.

Rush mats were used not only as rugs on the floor, but they were also hung up to serve as partitions in the house and spread out to be used as tables for serving meals. Special mats were made to wrap up ceremonial bundles. The old and worn mats served as a covering for the platform on which the family slept or rested when at home. They were also used when berrying or gathering wild rice. The mats could be easily rolled up for carrying or for storing when not in use. Though they are little used today, the rush mats are still made with straight line and diagonal designs worked out in colored rushes. Occasionally they are offered for sale. Old ones are to be found in many of the homes where they are valued as keepsakes from mothers and grandmothers.

Cattail Mats For Wigwams

Large cattail mats were used for covering the frames and lining the sides of the wigwams. In late summer when the cattails were full grown, the women gathered those that did not go to seed, wrapped them in bundles and dried them in the air. When the mats were made, the cattails were attached to a cord as when making rush mats. Basswood fiber that had been boiled to make it tough was threaded into a long bone needle and passed horizontally through the cattails at intervals of 8 or 10 inches. The needle was about

Plate 50   Wigwam of cat tail mats with roof of birch bark.

9 inches long and slightly curved. The eye of the needle was usually at one end, but sometimes it was near the center. The cattails were lapped in such a way that the threads were not visible. The lower ends of the warp were often left free so that only one side of the mat had a finish or selvage, and the mat could more easily rest in an upright position against the sides of the wigwam.

The lapping over of the cattails when sewed insured warmth and prevented water penetrating the lodge. Six mats were needed to cover the sides of a good sized dwelling. Twelve mats might be needed when a lodge was to be entirely covered by them. The cattail mats could be easily moved. The women would roll them in a big pack and put them on their backs to transport them from one place to another, as they followed their seasonal activities. There is little demand for such mats today, but the art of making them has not been entirely forgotten, and some are still being used.

Cedar Bark Mats

Where rushes were not abundant, mats were made chiefly of the inner bark of the red cedar (Juniperus virginana var. crebra Fernald and Griscom).

Plate 51.   An unfinished cedar bark mat.

The bark was gathered in the spring from the middle of May to the middle of June, according to the season. Strips about ¼ inch wide were prepared for both warp and weft. All strands are the same width. The natural color was a beautiful golden shade. Some strips were dyed black and brown with native dyes. A frame was used similar to that used when weaving rush mats. A wide variety of patterns was secured as the weaver carried one set of strips over one, two, or more of the other set of strips in different groupings and contrasting colors. As in making rush mats, it was necessary to keep the materials for the cedar bark mat damp and pliable while working, so that the woman usually sat in the shade to do her weaving. To finish the mat the edges were turned and "sewed over and over" with narrow strips of cedar bark. The cedar bark mats were used in summer on the floor, about the sides of the lodges, on the beds, as walls to divide the sleeping quarters and as doors. At meal time food was sometimes served on the cedar bark mats. Cedar bark mats are still being made by a few of the older women.

Woven Rag Rugs

For two or three generations the Ojibwa have been making a woven rug of rag strips using a simple heddle, but no shuttle, when doing the weaving. A similar heddle and method of weaving has been used in Germany and Italy and among the Zuni and a few other Indian tribes. The early colonists made use of such a heddle frame calling it a "tap-loom." The heddle is made of a cedar board about 13 inches square. Slits about one-half inch wide are cut across the board about one inch apart, leaving bars or slats each of which is pierced midway of its length by a heated wire which forms a small hole. When a rag rug is to be woven strips of cloth are passed through these holes. Other strips are passed between the bars. These two sets of cloth strips form the warp. One end of the warp strips is fastened firmly to a piece of furniture, while the other is secured to the worker's belt. The weft consists of a long strip of cloth wound in a roll to which additional strips are added as necessary. This roll is passed back and forth between the warp strands as the heddle is raised or lowered to change the relative position of the warp strands. Different patterns are secured in the bands by the use of different colors in the warp. Only one color is used in the weft. The number of bars in the heddle determines the possible number of warp strands. Narrower bands can be made as use is made of a fewer number of bars. The finished bands may be one and one-half inches or more in width. They are sewed together to form the round, oval, or oblong rugs that are frequently seen in the Ojibwa homes. In recent years similar bands have been made of yarn and carpet warp to serve as belts.

A few of the older women among the Minnesota Ojibwa have been

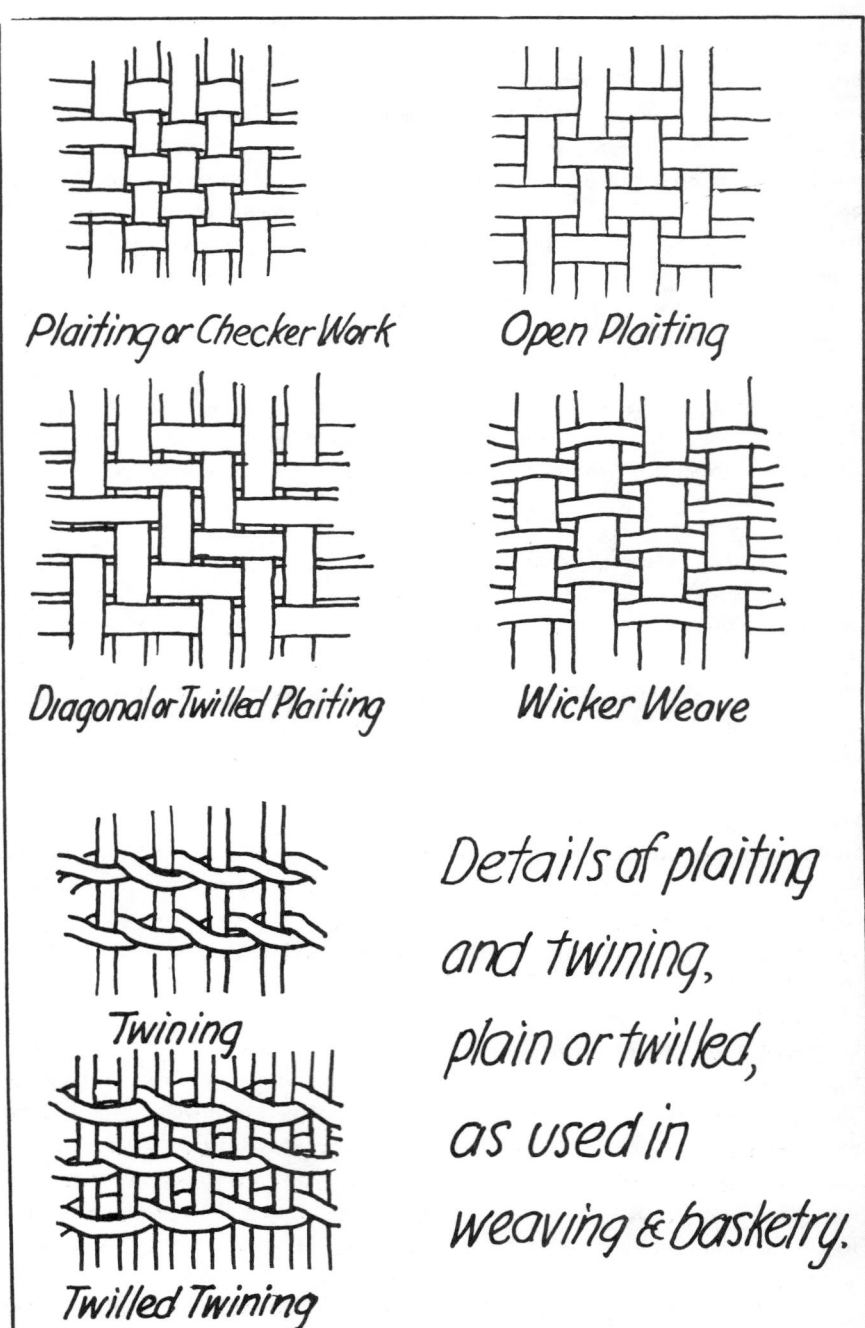

Plaiting or Checker Work

Open Plaiting

Diagonal or Twilled Plaiting

Wicker Weave

Twining

Twilled Twining

Details of plaiting and twining, plain or twilled, as used in weaving & basketry.

Plate 52.   Details of plaiting and twining.

making a durable and attractive rug of strips of rags, using the old twined techniques practiced in making the woven yarn bags, and working out designs similar to those used in the bags.

Braided rag rugs of modern type have been made by the Ojibwa for many years. The women are very skillful in making a flat braid with three or more strands of rag strips which they combine to form rugs of different shapes. More recently they have also made hooked rugs of rags, skillfully developing patterns with Ojibwa designs and scenes.

Plate 53.   A birchbark bitten pattern.

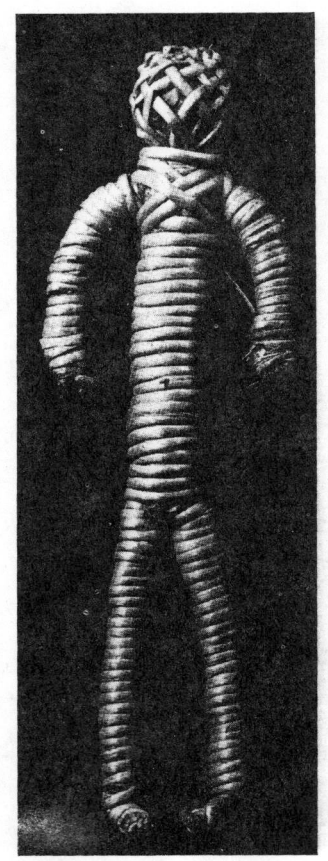

Plate 54. Doll made of
Willow withes.

PREPARATION AND USE OF HIDES

I N prehistoric days the Ojibwa men, women, and children wore clothing made of tanned hides of the deer, moose, caribou, bear, and elk. Delicately dressed skins of the rabbit, beaver, weasel, and other small animals were also used in the fashioning of their personal and ceremonial possessions. Drums, saddles, pouches, dance outfits, and many other articles were made of hides.

Tanning has always been a major industry of the Ojibwa women and has occupied much of their time. Even today in the homes of the older women on the wooded reservations, one frequently sees deer hides or the hides of some of the smaller animals being tanned as part of the day's work. In most localities all the hides are tanned that can be secured.

The native tanned hides vary in quality, color, and finish. Various methods of tanning have been practiced by different groups of Ojibwa to secure different grades of texture in the finished skins. Each worker has a method of tanning to which she adheres.

A good skin is uniform in thickness. Thin, soft skins are desired for most purposes. Buckskin is good material for clothing because it is warm, durable, and does not tear easily. Thick buckskin is chosen for moccasins and mittens. Doeskin is good for leggings and shirts, and fawnskin is used for fancy work. Skins of the unborn fawns are delicate and require much care in their preparation. They are used for the inner wrappings of war bundles and for other sacred articles.

In all the different methods of tanning buckskin (wawashkeshewaian, s., wawashkeshiwaianag, pl.) practiced by the Ojibwa on the various reservations the following steps or processes have been included: fleshing, dehairing, braining, stripping, graining, stretching, working or softening, and smoking. For each process the worker provided herself with a special type of tool which facilitated the work.

Fleshing.   The flesh side of the green hide is first cleaned by the use of a flesher. A primitive flesher was made by chiseling the narrow end of the shin bone (tibia) of the deer or moose, about six inches from the knee joint, to a slanting edge which is serrated. In the modern flesher a serrated iron blade is inserted. When the flesher is in use the knee joint end is loosely tied by a strip of buckskin to the wrist of the right arm of the worker and gripped so that the palm of the hand is toward the hide and the little finger is next to the serrated part. Strokes are taken away from the body.

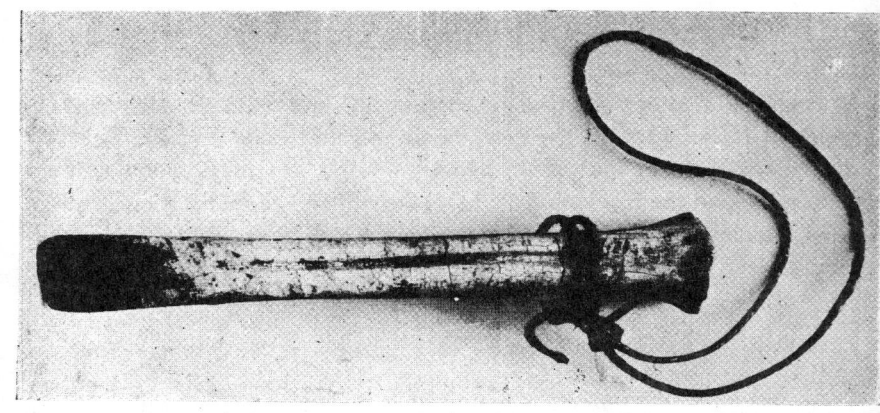

Plate 55.   Bone flesher for scraping hide.

Dehairing.   After the hide has been freed from adhering flesh, blood stains are washed off and the hide is soaked in clear water for some time. Some workers leave it in water for three days and three nights. Then it is wrung out vigorously and hung obliquely over an inclined log, the upper surface of which has been made smooth, or it is fastened to the branch of a tree and held taut with the left hand, and scraped to remove the hair and epidermis or surface skin. If the hair is very long, it is first cut off to facilitate the work of dehairing. The tool is pushed away from the worker against the grain of the hair. Scrapers were originally made from either the antler or the cannon bones of deer or elk.

Braining.   The next step is to soak the damp hide in a mixture of the brains of a deer or other large animal, and water. When a large animal is killed the brains are removed, spread out, dried, and saved for this purpose. To prepare them for use they are simmered in water to which a little fat has been added. If the hide is dry it is first softened in water, then the prepared brain mixture is spread on both sides and well rubbed in with the hands and a smooth stone until it is almost completely absorbed. Then the hide is sprinkled with warm water, rolled up tightly, and left over night. Then it is unrolled and sprinkled again with warm water and wrung out by grasping the head end of the hide in the right hand and tightly winding the hide around the right hand, wrist, and arm.

Stripping.   The hide is then thrown over a rod and both side are rolled up toward the center or back and the hide is twisted into a rope. This skin rope is placed around a tree, the ends are over-lapped and rolled together to secure them tightly, and a stout, smooth, round stick about three feet

Plate 56. Stretching and softening a buck skin.

in length is inserted and the roll is twisted tightly up to the tree, the stick being turned to one side, then to the other, wringing the moisture out of the skin and stretching it.

Scraping. After the hide has been stripped, it is unrolled and placed over a smooth, inclined log or "horse" to be scraped. The "horse" is fashioned by nailing one end of a smooth six-foot log to the vertex of two boards, the other end resting on the ground. Both sides of the hide are scraped with short strokes away from the body, the worker standing at the raised end of the horse, to remove any hair, flesh, or liquid that still adheres. The scraping is done with a rough stone or a modern scraper made by inserting a five-inch blade into a piece of oak nineteen inches long with seven-inch handles at each end.

Stretching. The hide has shrunken and become thickened by the preceding processes so that it is now necessary to restore it to the original size by pulling and stretching. Both the hands and feet are used in the stretching process. After the hides has been stretched in all directions holes are pierced along the entire edge about three inches apart, and the hide is attached to the poles of the stretching frame with leather thongs or basswood fiber so that it is taut.

The stretching frame has been made by nailing two horizontal rods one ten inches from the ground and the other nine inches from the upper ends of two vertical poles to form a frame about seventy-two by fifty-four inches according to the size of the skin.

Working and Softening.   The hair side of the skin is now subjected to a process of working or "beaming" to render it soft.

Today an iron implement eight inches long with a straight edge, one and one-half inches wide, bent at nearly right angles to the handle, like a hoe, is used as a beaming tool. Formerly a rock or an elk horn, with a blade of stone strapped to it with leather thongs, was used for the purpose. The left hand guides the scraper, while the right hand exerts pressure in such a way that the cellular filling is broken up, and the hide is softened. This treatment may require two or three hours. As the hide continues to stretch it is necessary to readjust it occasionally to keep it taut on the frame.

When the skin has become of even thickness, soft, pliable, absolutely dry, and no longer feels cold, it is ready for smoking. Any breaks or holes in the skin are repaired by patching and sewing them up with sinew inserted through holes made with an awl. The skin is white in color before being smoked. The smoking gives a cream, yellow, or tan color to the hide, and helps to protect it from destruction by moths and stiffening by water. After a smoked hide has been wet, it is possible with care to dry it so that it is soft and smooth.

Smoking.   Before being smoked the skin is sewed together with basswood or other fiber from head to tail in cylindrical shape to form a bag. The upper end is closed so that the bag is almost airtight and the smoke will fill the bag evenly. This skin bag is inverted over a long, tripod-like frame that has been erected over a shallow hole (about 1 foot wide and 6 inches deep) or the closed upper end is suspended from the branch of a tree or from a stick driven obliquely into the ground at an angle of about 45 degrees over the hole. The lower end of the bag is pegged or fastened down to the ground around the edge of the shallow hole in which a fire has been started. A small opening is tunnelled from one side to keep the fire supplied with air. When there is a good bed of coals, a smudge is secured by adding the soft inner bark of the pine tree, pine punk or other rotten wood, chips of green wood, crushed cedar bark, or birch bark packed with cones of the Norway or white pine. The fire must be watched carefully so that the skin is evenly smoked. When the inside of the bag has been smoked, it is reversed and the former outside is smoked, the smoking continuing until the pores are closed.

The time for smoking is not long, depending upon the thickness of the hide, the fuel used, and the results desired. A very thin hide might be smoked sufficiently in ten minutes. A thick hide might require an hour or more.

The color produced will range from a yellowish cream to a brownish tan, and is determined by the time allowed for the smoking, the kind of skin, and the wood used. White pine tends to make the skins black. Dried corn cobs are sometimes used, as they smoulder slowly and the smoke gives a golden yellow color.

The smoking produces the odor characteristic of Indian tanned hide. Dried willow twigs when burned produce a smoke with a strong odor. The smoke of rotten hemlock has very little odor. That from rotten cedar boughs has a pleasantly pungent odor. Each tanner has her favorite wood, from which she claims that the best results are obtained when smoking the hides. For some purposes the hides are not smoked, but are kept white. The smoked hides are folded up and laid away for a few days to set the color.

Bear hides (makówaian, s., makówaianag, pl.) to be used for bed coverings, mattresses, and floor mats, were scraped on the fleshy side, softened with a brain mixture and dried without removing the hair from the outer surface.

Rabbit Skin Blankets

Rabbit skins (wabosowaian, s., wabosowaianag, pl.) have been a great help to the Indians because of their soft fur. Today if they are to be used they are thoroughly soaked with wet salt, soda, and soap on the fleshy side, which is then gently rubbed and scraped. The hair is not removed.

Rabbit skin blankets were made by sewing the skins together, edge to edge. The furry side is used next to the body. Caps, neck scarfs, and wrappings for ankles and feet are worn with the hair inside.

Rabbit skin robes two inches thick and six feet square were made by sewing together full-length braids, each braid consisting of four three-inch strands of skin. Coats, hoods, and mittens were made by the same technique.

The Minnesota Ojibwa still make a delightfully soft and light blanket of rabbit skin strips without removing the hair or tanning the skin. The skins are gathered in winter after the hair of the rabbit has turned white. The whole skin may be stuffed with straw and hung for at least a month to allow the loose fur to be blown away, then cut circularly "round and round," in strips about one inch wide, which are loosely twisted in drying, forming a soft, thick fur cord. At Grand Portage the Indians cut the fresh skin in long strips which they hang at the top of long poles like banners, letting them blow in the wind as they dry and the hair is loosened from the skin. These long strips are tied or sewed together end to end, by a looping process with the skin strips running both ways. The strips are about one-half inch apart. As they cross, the strips are secured so that the blanket is firmly woven. The finished blanket is alike on both sides and is very thick and soft. For a large blanket six feet square as many as 100 rabbits are required. Rabbit skins were also used to line the cradle board, to put inside of children's moccasins, and for coats, mittens, hoods, neck scarfs and children's caps.

Bags of Skin

Bags of various kinds, for many different purposes, were made by the Ojibwa from the whole skins of the turtle, snake, mink ,and other small animals or from selected portions of the skins of large animals.

A stiff bag or box made from the whole foot of the deer with the hoof and hair left on is often seen in Ojibwa homes where it has served as an ornament as well as a useful container. A soft bag was also made of the deer's foot with the hoof left on for ornament.

Parfleche bags made of rawhide to serve for storage purposes, were used to some extent by the Plains Ojibwa but were not made by the Woodland Ojibwa.

Midé Bags. Of the bags made of whole skins with the hair left on, the most common example is the "midé bag." The midé bag was made of the skin of the beaver, mink, otter or weasel or of the wildcat paw or the bear paw. The skin was turned inside out, cleaned, and turned again so that it was in its natural form with the hair left on. Then it was stuffed with grass and dried. As it was to serve a ceremonial purpose it was ornamented with small pieces of bead weaving or embroidery. Decorative pieces were usually fastened to the paws, belly, and tail. Though the pieces were small, especially on the paws, and simple in design, the work was always carefully done, undoubtedly because the bags had ceremonial significance. When it was in use for the purpose it was to serve, the bag contained medicinal herbs, shells and charms, and was regarded as having special power. Every member of the Grand Medicine Society or Midéwiwin of the Ojibwa had such a bag. The bag was one of his most cherished possessions and was usually buried with him. As each degree of the society had a special type of bag it served as a distinctive badge showing the degree that had been attained by the owner. The bags were carefully stored away and only brought out for ceremonial use.

Pipe Bags. Bags of soft, tanned buckskin decorated with quills and beads were used for many purposes. Among these the tobacco bag or pipe bag

Plate 57.   Midé bag (beaver skin medicine bag).

is probably the most distinctive. It had an important place among the Indians. The Ojibwa carried the pipe bag on special occasions when the ceremonial costume was worn. The bag was about eighteen inches long by six inches wide with a fringe 6 inches or more in length. The lower 6 inches of the bag was often decorated with very fine quill or bead work in which distinctive tribal designs were used. Fringe cut from buckskin was used to decorate the side seams as well as the bottom of the bag. The Ojibwa pipe bag was not so large nor so elaborately decorated as were the pipe bags of the Sioux.

Moccasins (makisin, s., makisinan, pl.)

The early moccasins of the Woodland Indians were made of deer or moose hide and were of the one-piece, soft-soled, pucker-top type. Seams at the instep and heel served to shape the moccasin. The seam up the front was gathered or puckered. It was often covered with a strip of quill weaving or embroidery and separate pieces of skin were added as cuffs at the top of the moccasin. The later Ojibwa usually added a yoke or vamp as well as fold-down cuffs to the one piece lower part. Sometimes the cuffs were fringed. A tongue, notched at the free end, was usually added to the vamp. One large buckskin would make as many as nine pairs of men's moccasins. Moccasins for infants and old women were sometimes made of two pieces of leather

Plate 58.   Old puckered toe moccasins embroidered in yarn.

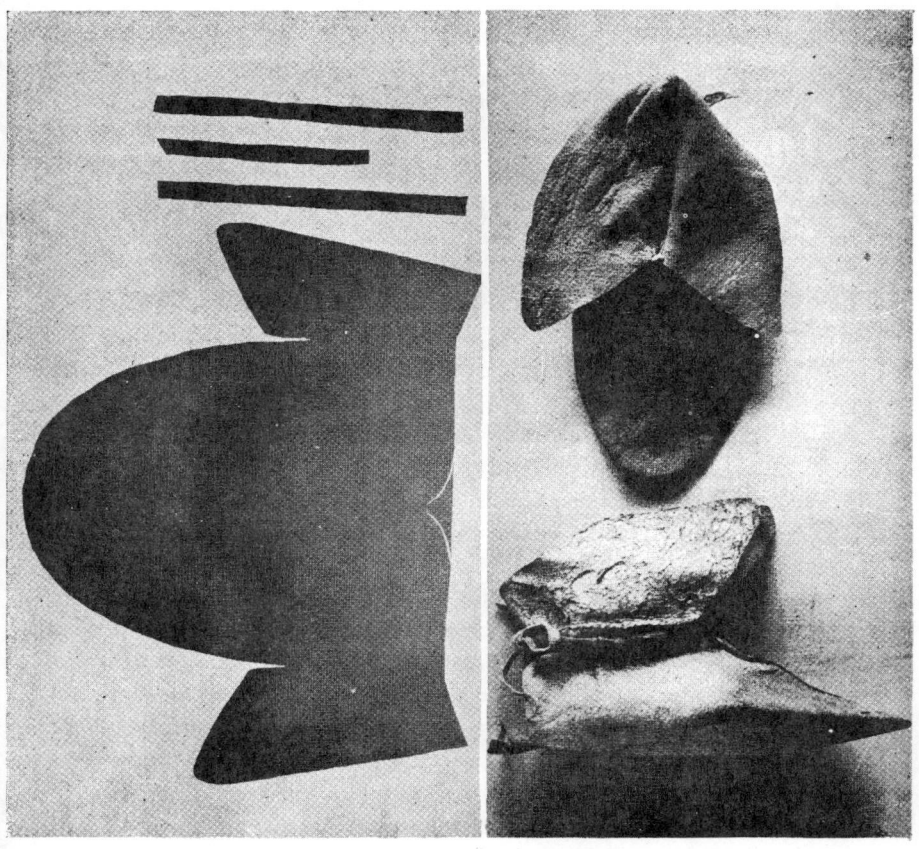

Plate 59.   Moccasin pattern (old style) and finished moccasin.

with a seam extending the length of the sole and up the front and back of the foot.

The moccasin in early days was sewed up with thread prepared from cedar bark or with sinew taken from the large back tendon of the deer. These native fibers long ago gave place in sewing to thread supplied by the trader.

The soft-soled Ojibwa moccasin of buckskin was made for comfort and was less highly decorated than were the heavily beaded moccasins of the Sioux. The center yoke and turned over cuff of the Ojibwa moccasin afforded effective space for simple quill and bead work designs. Cut-out patterns, designs based on the double curve, and simple realistic floral designs, have been used as moccasin decorations both on the yoke and the cuffs.

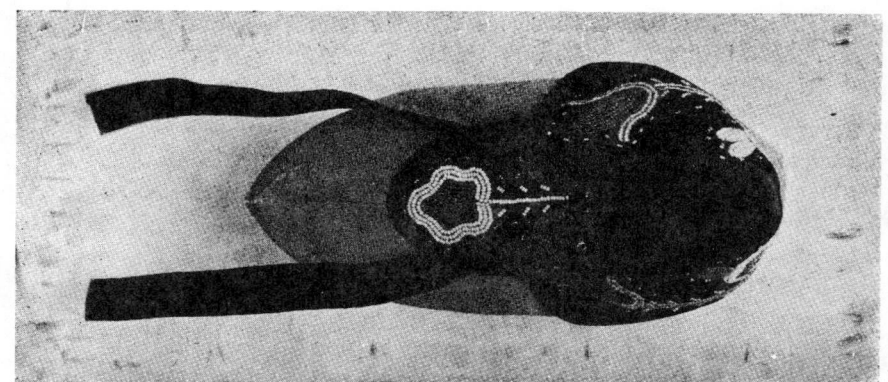

Plate 60.   Modern moccasin with beaded velvet top.

In making the later moccasins, velvet was often used for the yoke and cuffs. These were decorated with heavy floral designs in bead embroidery. The yoke and cuffs thus embroidered were often transferred from old moccasins to new ones and used many times.

Children's moccasins have sometimes been decorated with a dainty design worked out in chain stitch with sewing thread. This method of decorating buckskin goes back to an early date. In winter, before the child's moccasin was worn, it was filled with the down of the cat-tail rushes to provide additional warmth.

The Ojibwa followed the custom of the Winnebago, Cherokee, and Seneca, perforating the sole of the child's moccasin so that the child could not be enticed away by the spirits, the moccasin giving the appearance of being in too poor a condition to undertake a long journey.

COSTUMES

Woman's Costume
(matchigoden, s., matchigodenian, pl. or godass, s., godassan, pl.)

THE woman's early costume consisted of a single sleeveless garment made of two deer skins—one skin forming the front and the other the back. They were fastened together over the shoulders by strips of skin and held in place by a belt. From the belt hung ornaments and trinkets. One deer skin was sufficient for the child's dress. The woman's dress was worn over an underskirt of woven nettle fiber. She also wore leggings and moccasins and an

Plate 61.   An Ojibwa girl in costume of 1850.

outer robe of skin with or without fur, for which the blanket was later substituted. Her leggings were wide and lapped over several inches at the side. They extended a few inches above the knee, but were fastened below the knee with a band or leather thong. Her hair was worn long, usually braided or bound in a queue.

Later the skin dress was made with the upper edge of the skin turned down or finished with small rectangular flaps. Deep notches were cut at the top for arm pits. Two straps were attached to the upper edge to go over the

Plate 62.　Women's Leggings.

shoulders. The straps and the flaps across the front and back were usually decorated with quill or bead work: Separate sleeves were open from the elbow up. They were fastened together with a string and under the chin.

When broadcloth became available during the latter part of the 17th century the Ojibwa woman made use of it for her leggings and principal garment, cutting the latter in much the same form as the skins which had made up her primitive dress. Red, dark blue, and black broadcloth were most commonly used. The broadcloth costume was worn on social and ceremonial

Plate 63.   Women's leggings.

Plate 64.   A modern Ojibwa girl in old time costume.

occasions. For some years the costume of skins continued to be used as a work dress. Eventually it was replaced by calico in solid colors or figured patterns.

The broadcloth garment, made after the fashion of the skin dress, passed rather loosely around the body and was held in place by straps over the shoulder and a belt or girdle about the waist. The straps and girdle were often elaborately decorated. Separate arm coverings or sleeves were made of two strips of cloth, each fastened at the wrist like a cuff and attached to one another at the back, forming a cape-like protection to the shoulders. Sometimes in place of the arm coverings the women wore a loose calico sacque quite different from any contemporary garment of their White neighbors, undoubtedly modeled after an earlier Indian one made of skin.

Simple border designs of beads provided the decoration on the early cloth dresses. The zigzag or otter tail patterns were often embroidered in white beads across the yoke and straps. On the later broadcloth dresses, border decorations of silk ribbon work or applique were used. Silk ribbons were available from the early eighteenth century.

During the latter half of the nineteenth century when velveteen came into use among the Ojibwa it was made up into an elaborate dress with a full skirt decorated with the same large beaded floral designs that were used on the men's breech cloths, leggings, cuffs, yokes, vests, and jackets of the period. Only a few of these velveteen dresses are to be seen today. Their use was probably never universal because of the high price of the materials. One may sometimes be seen at a ceremonial or dance, or in a museum collection. Old beaded costumes are treasured in many homes.

At the present time the distinctive dress worn by the Ojibwa women of Minnesota at their dances is a full, black cotton dress decorated with bright colored ribbons, metal disks, and ruffles on which there is a metal fringe. The jingle of the metal fringe is designed to contribute, when the wearer is moving, to the rhythm of the dance music.

Neither the velveteen dress nor the present day dance costume bears any apparent relation to the native skin costume of 200 years ago.

Man's Costume (agwiwin, s., agwiwinan, pl.)

The earliest recorded costume for the Ojibwa man consisted of skin breech cloth, leggings, moccasins, and a buckskin robe. For the skin robe a commercially woven blanket obtained from the trader was soon substituted. The early blankets were usually white, red, green, sky-blue, or indigo blue. At first they were worn gracefully draped from the shoulders. At one time they were formed into a loose coat with a hood, and were held in place by means of a belt (kitchipison, s., kitchipisonan, pl.). The hood was pulled up in bad weather. To it a feather was sometimes added for decoration. The colored stripes and selvage on the blanket served to ornament it. This wrap was used only by the men and boys, not by girls and women.

Broadcloth and calico came into early use in the costume of the man as well as of the woman. Schoolcraft in his Personal Memoirs describes the Ojibwa chiefs at a meeting held in Sault Sainte Marie, July 9, 1822, as follows, "The other chiefs observed their native costume, which is, with this tribe, a toga of blue broadcloth folded and held by one hand on the breast, over a light figured calico shirt, red cloth leggings, and beaded moccasins, a belt or baldaric about the waist sustaining a knife sheath and pouch, and a frontlet of skin, or something of the sort, around the forehead, environed generally with eagles' feathers."

The man's hair was worn as long as it would grow and braided. When going on the warpath the head was decorated with a scalp lock. To make the scalp lock, three small wisps of hair, the amount growing on a space about the size of a silver half dollar, were taken up on the crown of the head and braided, the braid being firmly tied midway the length of the hair and wrapped with moosewood, basswood or other strong bark so that it would stand erect on the head for six or eight inches. The hair above the braid was allowed to fall over, giving the lock a parasol appearance. After cloth came into use, bright red flannel was used on the braid in place of the bark as the warrior desired to make scalp lock as conspicuous as possible.

Caps of burdock leaves (Arctium minus Bernh), turbans of otter skin, peaked hoods, and a headgear combined with a long mantle made of cloth (a capote) have been worn as head covering by the Ojibwa at different periods. A folding cap, similar to the cap of the Scots soldier and the veteran's cap of the A. E. F. made of velvet of broadcloth and often richly beaded, was used by the men during the latter part of the last century. In 1860 the men were still wrapping their heads with a strip of fur or a woven cloth worn in the form of a turban. The woven yarn sash was often used for this purpose. To this head band one or more eagle feathers were added, usually at one side near the back.

The eagle feather tipped with red flannel or with horse hair dyed red, worn in the hair, is familiar in pictures of the Ojibwa. It was an evidence of great personal bravery and was not a mere decoration. It could only be worn by one who had met the enemy or secured a scalp, one feather for each scalp. Many feathers gave evidence that an indefinite number of persons had been scalped. A split feather indicated that the wearer has been wounded by an enemy. A large red spot on a feather indicated that the wearer had been wounded by a bullet. If eagle feathers could not be obtained, wild turkey

Plate 65.   An Ojibwa man in ceremonial costume.

feathers were worn in the hair. Horns were sometimes used in front of the head dress as an emblem of power and chieftancy.

For over 400 years a roach headdress of dyed animal hair has been made by the Ojibwa men and worn by them going to war, at their feasts and dances, and on other special occasions. The roach was usually made of stiff moose hairs or porcupine hairs 6 or 8 inches in length combined with the softer white hair (3 or 4 inches long) from the deer's tail dyed a brilliant red. Today horse hairs are often used in making the roach. The stiff hairs stand erect when the roach is worn on the head.

To construct the roach a long cord is strung on a bow loom from 8 to 10 inches across and to this the hairs are attached to form a fringe. The end of the cord to which the fringe has been attached is then wound about to form a small circle from which a strip of the cord is allowed to extend for 6 or 8 inches, according to the size of the wearer, and doubled back on itself, the parallel cords being stitched together. Successive turns of the cord are made around the circle and tail, enlarging them. Each successive row or turn of the cord is stitched to the previous one.

When worn, the roach is fastened to the head by pulling the scalp lock through a hole that is left in the circular part and tying it firmly. Today leather thongs are used to secure the head dress if the scalp lock is not worn. A long feather is often so attached to the circular portion of the head dress as to rotate freely. When the roach is not in use the end of a long stick is inserted in this hole and the hairs that make up the roach are carefully wrapped around the stick, tied down, and covered with a soft skin or cotton cloth for protection.

The Ojibwa used color on their faces. In the early days the cheeks and forehead were tattooed in different colors. The faces of the warriors were covered with vermilion. As late as 1866 they covered their backs with white clay, and after it had dried and hardened, adhering to the skin, painted on it all sorts of curious designs.

The men's leather leggings extended from the ankle almost to the hips and were held in place by a leather thong tied to a belt. They were not so wide as the women's leggings and did not lap over so far at the side. A band or thong tied below the knee helped to hold them in place.

After the introduction of commercially woven materials the leggings were usually made of velveteen or broadcloth and the band at the knee was replaced by a quilled or beaded band or a woven yarn garter. Both the embroidered bands and the yarn garters were finished at each end with a long yarn fringe to be used in tying them around the knee. The velvet leggings were usually ornamented with floral designs in bead embroidery or with silk

Plate 66.   Roach headdress on stick (a) as worn (b) as stored away.

Plate 67. Man's leggings.

ribbon work. The velvet breech cloth and the jacket and cuffs that came into use in the costume of a later period were similarly decorated. An elaborately beaded yoke that fits flat around the neck, and usually extends across the shoulders and down the front, has formed the upper part of the modern ceremonial shirt.

Costume Decorations and Accessories

At different periods in the history of the Ojibwa various articles and materials have been used to embellish their costumes and other personal articles. At an early date delicate designs were embroidered in moose hair on both skins and birch bark. Moose hair embroidery was done on black velvet

Plate 68.   Beaded breechcloth.

Plate 69.   Beaded breechcloth.

up to 1845. Commercial sewing thread was used in much the same way. Colored grasses have also been used in the embroidery work, their shiny surface resembling that of quills. Much of the early decoration on costumes and personal articles consisted of quill work applied to the skins with embroidery stitches taken with sinew. The early Ojibwa did not make so much use of the

117

Plate 70.   Beaded sash and headbands.

elaborate quilled fringes and strips of plaited quill work as did the Plains Indians nor did they use the woven techniques as much with quills as they did with beads. As the nineteenth century advanced, quill work was gradually replaced by bead work until it died out almost entirely. Beads have been popular with the Ojibwa, both in weaving and in embroidered patterns on skins and cloth, ever since the traders first brought beads to the Great Lakes region.

The designs used on the various articles that made up the man's costume differed in character and use from those on the early costumes of the women. The large floral pattern that has been used so generally on the man's costume during recent years occurs only on the late velvet or velveteen trimmed costumes of the women. The white beading on the earlier broadcloth dresses was used in combination with more elaborate designs on the pouches carried by the men.

Plate 71.   Ojibwa pouches with bandoliers in geometric and floral designs.

Though less given to memorializing the deeds of valor of their warriors by the use of symbolic decorations than were the war-like Sioux, the Ojibwa took much pride in their appearance during the ceremonies of the Midéwiwin Society and presented a festive appearance when they wore their ceremonial costumes decorated with colored quill and bead embroidery, highly colored yarn or bead sashes, and beaded shoulder pouches or bandoliers.

Ceremonial occasions continue to demand the handsomely decorated costumes and the colorful costume accessories for a few members of the tribe. Such articles are also valued as gifts, exchanges of beaded articles being prompted by friendship or by personal obligations. Often a choice piece of quill or bead work is given by the original owner to someone to whom he is indebted and by whom it is sure to be highly prized even though it may be no longer worn.

For many years buckskin jackets and gloves have been made by the Ojibwa for trade purposes. The demand for such articles has been increasing with the increased interest in winter sports in the Great Lakes region. The women apparently continue to enjoy working with the native material even though they fashion them to meet modern needs.

QUILL WORK

A MONG the arts early practiced by the Woodland Indians was the use of quills for decorative purposes. The quills commonly used in craft work were those of the porcupine, but at one time some use was made of bird quills. The porcupine quills (kagobiwai, s., kagobiwaian, pl.) are white, tipped in brown, and the Indian craft workers arranged them so as to form interesting patterns. Additional colors were secured by dyeing the quills with native dyes, and their use added to the beauty of the quill patterns.

Porcupine quill work had developed to a high degree of artistic perfection before the first European explorers reached this country. It was carried on almost universally by the Indians who inhabited Canada and the northeastern and north central sections of the United States and to some extent by Indians in the wooded section of the south where porcupines were abundant. Specimens of very fine work, many of them known to be at least 200 years old, have been collected. Complicated techniques were used in the old work. In later years the work has not been so fine nor have the techniques been as varied.

Quills were plaited or braided, woven, wrapped to form stiff fringes and other decorative strips, used to form borders and unit designs on birch bark articles, or applied to tanned skins with embroidery stitches made with sinew. The plaited quill work and the ornamental fringes were much used by the Plains Indians. Along the northern shores of the Great Lakes among the Canadian Indians quills were woven into bands and strips to be used in costume decoration. A few old pieces of quill weaving have been attributed to the Ojibwa, but it is doubtful whether the Ojibwa to the south of the Great Lakes practiced much quill weaving. The Ojibwa in Minnesota and Wisconsin have no such tradition.

In the early days the Ojibwa did some fine embroidery work with quills (onagaskwawai, s., onagaskwawaian, pl.) on soft buckskin and the softer fawn skin. The finest quill work closely resembles the moose hair embroidery which was carried on at an early date, on both birch bark and buckskin.

Colored grasses were sometimes used in the same way, their shiny surface resembling that of quills. At a later time sewing thread was used in working out fine embroidery patterns similar to the early quill decorations. After the introduction of glass beads, the art of quill embroidery work gradually declined and it has been little practiced in recent years.

Quill Work On Birch Bark

Quilled designs were worked out on birch bark with a simple technique which is still being practiced by the Ojibwa in Michigan and Minnesota and to a more limited extent in Wisconsin. At Grand Portage, Minnesota, many of the well made birch bark bowls, boxes, and waste baskets are decorated with effective quill designs applied as borders and as unit designs both in the natural colors and in the brighter dyed colors. A few of the craft workers at Cass Lake, Minnesota, also use quills in decorating birch bark containers. The quills used in much of the birch bark work are coarse, and the work is not so fine as that done in the early days.

A stencil or cut pattern is sometimes used for making the birch bark decorations. Before the quills are applied, a pattern is outlined on the bark by the used of a blunt pointed bone marker. Such outlines are seldom found on the articles made by the early craft workers who did not rely on patterns.

When quill work is done on birch bark the quills are soaked in water until soft. The sharp ends of unflattened quills are inserted from the back through small holes made in the birch bark by an awl shaped from an antler or a bone of an elk or deer. The awl is somewhat smaller in diameter than the quills. The quills are drawn through the hole from the back to the front, bent over, and carried parallel and close to the birch bark surface to another hole through which the sharp end is drawn to the back of the bark surface. The ends of the quills are trimmed off, bent and pressed close to the back of the bark where they dry and thus serve as a fastening for the quill. The quills dry and stiffen, and the holes in the bark seem to contract after the quill ends have been inserted, thus holding the quill securely. It is not necessary to fasten the quills down with sinew or other thread. When the exterior of a container is decorated with quilled designs, a thin lining of birch bark with a scalloped edge is usually provided to cover the ends of the quills that show on the inside of the container. (See frontispiece).

Quill Embroidery

When a quill embroidery pattern was to be worked out on skin, stitches were taken with threads of sinew around which the quills were folded to fasten them to the skin. The sinew was secured from the tendon that runs down the back of the deer or other large animal. The tendon was cleaned and dried, then separated into fine threads sometime before the work was to begin. These threads of sinew had considerable strength. Old pieces of quill work that have been sewed with sinew have kept in good condition through the years.

Three types of stitches were used,—a running or spot stitch, a back stitch, and a button hole or loop stitch. The stitches were taken from left to right of the pattern and were caught only through the upper surface of the skin in a hole made by a pointed bone or metal awl. The sinew was never carried through the skin from back to front except to hold the knotted ends so that no stitches appeared on the wrong side of the embroidered piece. Passing the sinew only through the surface made it possible to take the fine stitches characteristic of the early quill work with the delicate floral designs.

The quills were well washed, preferably in a soapy bath before being used. While working, the woman usually kept a few quills moist by holding them in her mouth, sometimes with points protruding, and pulled them out as needed. As she pulled them out she flattened them between her teeth and her thumb and forefinger. The heat of the mouth as well as the moisture was effective in softening the quills. It was thought that the saliva contained some special property that made them more pliable.

The moistened quills were caught under and folded over the sinew. The stitch was never taken through the quill since the quill would have split if the awl had been run through it. Good quill embroidery was characterized by the fact that the sinew stitches did not show, since they did not pass through the back of the skin, and in front they were concealed by the quills that passed over them.

An antler, a smooth flat bone or a specially designed iron instrument known as a "quill flattener" was used by some of the women to flatten the quills after the embroidered design had been completed, but flattening with the fingernails was usually sufficient to produce a smooth result. (For further discussion of quill technique see "Quill and Beadwork of the Western Sioux," Indian Handcrafts, No. 1.)

BEAD WORK

BEADWORK, both woven and embroidered, followed quill work in the early decorations of a great variety of bags, moccasins and other personal articles made of skin. At a later period embroidery work with glass beads (manitóminen, s., manitóminensag, pl.) was done on broadcloth, velveteen, and other commercially woven materials, with commercial thread.

During the 18th century glass beads were common articles of trade between the Indians and the early settlers all the way from New York to the Rocky Mountains. As early as 1711 glass beads were being used in the region which is now Michigan. By 1780 great quantities of beads were being sold through the British trading posts to the Indians dwelling around the Great Lakes. In recent excavations on the site of the old trading post that flourished at Grand Portage from 1780 to 1800, thousands of glass and porcelain beads of various colors, sizes and shapes have been found. Among them are large seed beads chiefly in white and light blue. A few are deep red in color.

The fine white seed beads which were used by the Iroquois all through the 18th century probably came into use among the Ojibwa during the latter part of the century or early in the 1800's. The Ojibwa used the opaque seed beads in a variety of colors, exercising much care in their selection and combination. The seed beads are partially handmade, hence somewhat irregular in shape, varying in size from one-sixteenth to three-sixteenths of an inch in diameter. Today the women do not use as fine a bead as they did in the 19th century.

Transluscent beads began to be used by the Ojibwa about sixty years ago (1860) but the seed beads have always been the more popular. The very fine transluscent beads are no longer obtainable at the traders stores and old collections of these beads are carefully treasured to be used on choice pieces that are to serve a special purpose.

Some of the best and most characteristic pieces of quill and bead weaving and embroidery were those made for the decoration of the midé bags. A similar type of embroidered bead decoration was used on the sacred drum. Saddle covers were sometimes elaborately quilled and beaded.

Bead Weaving

Bead weaving on a simple loom is an art that has been practiced by the Ojibwa for many years. In the early weaving, the work was done with threads of sinew strung on a weaving bow fashioned from the branch of a shrub. A double piece of birch bark in which holes had been made, was used to separate the threads of sinew. The simple birch bark heddle has continued in use among the older women, being easy to make and carry with them. Elaborate heddles were at one time introduced by the Jesuits but there is no evidence that they were ever in general use. The Sauk, Fox, Potawatomi, Menomini, Micmac and Winnebago also made some use of heddles. Old heddles, elaborately decorated, are shown in the museums.

Early bead frames were made of ash, tied with sinew at the corners, and were usually square. Modern bead looms are small wooden frames usually oblong.

To do the weaving the loom is strung by winding linen thread tightly around it from one end to the other, to serve as the warp. The threads must be evenly spaced and the warp kept taut. One more warp thread is used than the number of beads required across the design.

Linen or silk thread is used for the weft. A very fine, long bead needle is used to carry the weft thread. After the needle has been threaded, one end of the weft is tied to the left end of the warp threads. Enough beads are strung on the threaded needle to reach across the width of the design (one less than the number of warp threads).

The string of beads is passed under the warp threads from the left and

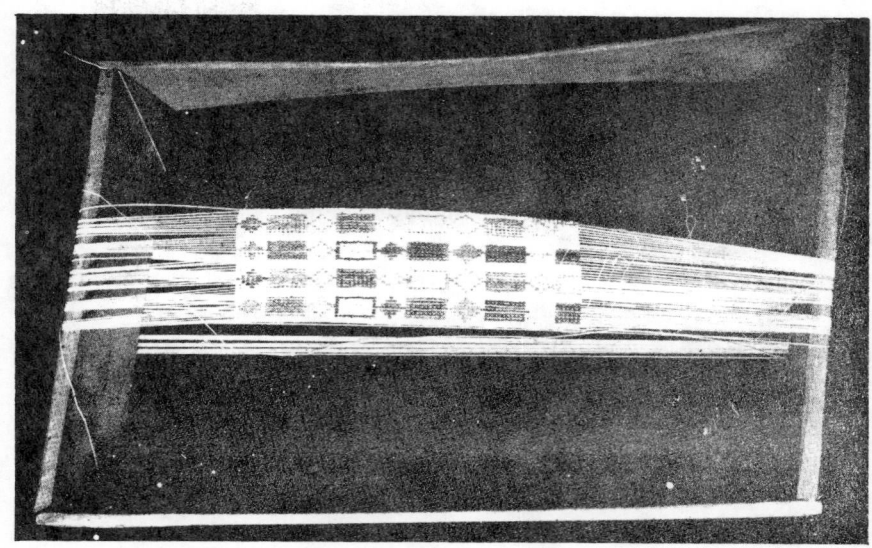

Plate 72. Beaded band being woven on a simple loom.

124

a bead is pushed up between each two warp threads. The beads are held in place with the left hand while the needle is inserted from the right and again passed through the beads this time so that it will carry the weft thread over the warp threads. Each succeeding row of beads is added in the same way. When the woven piece is finished it is taken from the loom and the warp threads are tied together to prevent the band from unravelling.

Bead Embroidery

In bead embroidery the Ojibwa have used a different technique from the Sioux and the finished pieces of the two tribes differ distinctively from one another. The Sioux bead workers used the lazy stitch which gives to their work a ridged appearance. The bead embroidery of the Ojibwa is smoothly done with the "spot" or "couched" stitch, the design often being worked out against a background of solid white beading. In using the couched stitch the beads are strung on a thread of sinew and then laid in position according to color and design and the first thread is overlaid or "couched" down by a second thread at irregular intervals, usually after each two beads. This holds the beads down firmly and in a solidly beaded pattern gives a fine mosaic effect when well done. In the old bead work the stitch was not carried through the skin so that the under side was free of stitches.

The early bead embroidery on skins was all done with sinew and was much stronger than that which is made today with ordinary commercial thread. Among the Woodland Indians moose and deer were the chief sources of sinew. Moose sinew was rather coarse and was kept for heavy work but the deer sinew could be split into exceedingly fine strands and used for fine sewing and with fine beads. After the introduction of woven textiles, broadcloth and velvet became the basis for most of the bead embroidery, and commercial thread supplanted sinew for sewing.

Beaded Border Patterns

In the early Ojibwa beadwork carried on in the latter part of the 18th and the early part of the 19th centuries, much use was made of white beads by sewing and couching them on skin or cloth in a straight line, a zigzag, an otter tail, or other simple geometric pattern. Occasionally a curved or festooned design was used in the border pattern. These early simple designs contrast strikingly with the heavily beaded floral designs that came into use between the years 1860-1870 after the Ojibwa had seen the floral designs that were being used by the French in their chintzes and elaborate laces. The simple border designs continued in use after the floral design had been developed and often the two styles are to be found on the same piece of work.

125

Plate 73.   Beaded velvet bag with four tabs.

Sometimes the border patterns were used as a finish to the silk applique or ribbon work which was used by the Ojibwa to some extent.

The simple border patterns are of ancient origin and were popular in all the old Algonquin quill work. The Iroquois and other eastern tribes made use of them in their early work, but later elaborated them, introducing scrolls and double curves and working out a wide border pattern more complicated than were the border patterns of the Ojibwa.

The beaded border patterns were the only decoration on the broadcloth and cotton dresses worn at one period by the Ojibwa women. They were also used on the band wrapped around the baby cradle. Frequently they were used to fill in a large space on a bag or other article, row after row being worked in repetition.

Beaded Edging

The Ojibwa, in common with other tribes, made an edging usually of white beads to finish the outer seams of many of their beaded bags and bands. In making this bead edging the thread is passed through a bead then

OLD DESIGNS USED IN BEADWORK

Plate 74. Embroidered bead border designs.

ihrough the material and up through the bead again. Two other beads are then threaded before the thread again passes through the material and up again through the third bead. When the stitch is taken and the thread drawn tightly the central bead remains in a horizontal position but the two beads that are fastened down on each side assume a vertical position, thus giving an attractive edge or finish to the seam with the beads alternately vertical and horizontal.

Plate 75.   Beaded band.

Beaded Bands and Sashes

After European beads had become plentiful, beaded bands of varying widths were woven in elaborate designs to be worn as a purely decorative part of the costume either across the shoulders or around the belt. The largest of these bands are from six to eight inches in width and from 1½ to 2 yards in length. After being woven they were often mounted on a belt of leather, heavy drill or other lining so that they could be used without being injured. The ends were finished with a deep yarn fringe which was braided or hung free. Smaller bands, two inches by eighteen inches and four inches by twenty inches, showing equally interesting designs, were also made for garters, head bands, and other parts of the costume. Strands of yarn two feet or more in length hung from the ends of the garters to tie them about the knee. Bands four inches wide and ten or more inches in length were woven with elaborate designs worked out in both seed beads and transluscent glass beads. These short, wide bands were apparently worn as a breast decoration, for some of them are provided with a narrow neck band woven with beads. The beaded bands show some of the most attractive designs used by the Ojibwa during recent years.

Shoulder Pouches or Bandoliers

One of the most striking articles in the ceremonial costume of the Ojibwa is the ceremonial bag, a large beaded pocket with shoulder band. Such bags have been used since colonial days. Worn by the well-to-do on ceremonial occasions it seems to be as popular today as it was a generation ago. An Ojibwa wearing a beaded pouch is considered in full dress. Two pouches were often worn, one on each shoulder. The shoulder pouch or bandolier resembled the pocket or bullet pouch decorated with a crest which was worn by the British soldier about the middle of the eighteenth century. Since its adoption by the Ojibwa and other Woodland tribes, it has become more highly decorated. The Ojibwa were making the beaded pouch in the early years of the nineteenth century. It is said that at that time, when winter was over, pouches that had been beaded by the Ojibwa were carried to the Sioux country to be exchanged for ponies. Each beadwork pouch was worth a pony.

The pouch consists of a large square case or bag about 18 inches by 18 inches, with a broad band or baldric long enough to go around the neck so that the pouch hangs almost to the knees. Both the pouch and the band are highly decorated with bead weaving or embroidery. Sometimes the woven square and band are all in one piece, with designs that harmonize. From a study of the early pouches on which the woven beadwork was used, one can find some of the geometric motifs most frequently employed by the Ojibwa.

About 1860 when beads became available in great quantities, the Ojibwa began to decorate their pouches with all-over bead embroidery, using beads of many colors in large floral patterns.

Plate 76.   Beaded band.

At one time the embroidered patterns on the shoulder pouches were done against a black velveteen background. This may have been due to a scarcity of beads, for the Ojibwa seem to have preferred the solid beading as a background. In some cases the upper part of the pouch was of black velveteen with a single or double row of beads outlining a floral design, while the lower part was solidly beaded. A slit between the back and front provided an opening to the pouch, though little use seems to have been made of it as a container. In some cases the bag has even been replaced by a beaded square.

At the bottom of the Ojibwa shoulder pouches there usually hangs a row of a dozen or more woven strips of beading about 1 inch wide and 6 inches in length ending in a woolen tassel. The strips at one side of the middle may each show different geometric designs which are repeated in the other half from the center out. In the old bags these strips were woven in the same piece with the square, extending their length beyond the square. On some bags large bone beads were used to make the fringe. In one handsome museum piece (Denver) the fringe is made up of strands of beads braided together, six strands to the braid. Some of the smaller bags made of velveteen have four or five rounded tabs of the material, attractively embroidered, left on in place of the fringe.

Curious contrasts in colors, designs, and materials occur in these old beaded pouches. Beads in three or four shades of blue, two shades of green, brown and tan. and pink and red were often used on the same piece. Sometimes two or more unrelated designs are shown on the shoulder band. Not only are many colors and various types of bead work and of design used in the same pouch, but often the color of the beads will change abruptly as the design is being worked out—probably because of a change in the supply of beads available. The finished shoulder pouches and their bands are usually lined with calico or with a heavy ticking and are bound with woolen braid.

Plate 77.   Knife sheath with porcupine quill decoration.

RIBBON WORK OR APPLIQUE

IN common with other Woodland Indians, the Ojibwa used silk ribbon work, applied by the method commonly known as applique, in making borders to decorate their broadcloth costumes. However, they accepted the European costume at so early a date that they did not develop ribbon work to such a high art as did the Potawatomi and other tribes which continued to wear the native Indian costume until a much later date.

Ribbons in bright colors were being used by the Indians of the Great Lakes early in the eighteenth century (1711). By the early part of the nineteenth century they were being used in applique designs. At first the designs were simple, straight-line border patterns then diamond, hexagon, zigzag, and checker-board patterns developed in the borders. The Ojibwa made much use of these simple, straight-line patterns. Though they later developed some graceful curvilinear patterns their work does not show the elaborate floral patterns of the Winnebago, Potawatomi, Menomini, Sauk, and Fox. By the latter part of the nineteenth century ribbon work was being used as a border on robes and leggings, as decorations on the binding bands of cradle boards, and on the cuffs and front pieces of moccasins.

To make a ribbon work border, two pieces of ribbon in contrasting color of light and dark were selected. Either narrow or wide ribbons were used for the work, as the surface to be covered demanded. Several rows of ribbon were sometimes required. The first ribbon served as a background. It was usually placed over a piece of calico to give it body. A design was cut from the second piece of ribbon. This was laid on the first ribbon and sewed to it with the very finest of briar or catch stitches, or with a blind stitch, such as is used on hems. Sometimes a border of white beads was added as a finish. The thread used for the briar stitch was usually in contrasting color to the ribbon. A very fine steel needle was used in doing the work.

The designs to be used in ribbon work were usually cut out free hand. In some cases a paper pattern was first made. As the paper was often folded before cutting, many of the patterns were symmetrical.

The pattern was repeated as many times as necessary to fill the width and length of the ribbon border. It was sometimes worked out in four colors, light and dark shades alternating.

DESIGNS

Designs On Woven Mats, Bags, and Sashes

WORKING as they did in many different media, the Ojibwa developed different types of designs. Some of the oldest designs of the tribe are to be seen on their old cedar bark and rush mats, woven bags, and yarn sashes. Most of these old designs are geometric, controlled in large measure by the processes of weaving involved. They include straight line and zigzag borders, hexagons, squares, diamonds, and triangles, usually elongated and arranged against a background of contrasting shade or color. The artistic sense of the Ojibwa is indicated in the choice and arrangement of the patterns and colors.

Combined with the geometric designs, conventionalized animal figures representing the deer, the panther, the turtle, and the thunder bird are to be found on the old nettle fiber bags. These may have been tribal designs or dream symbols having religious significance.

Triangular, zigzag, and arrow patterns occurred on the woven yarn sashes.

Designs on Quill Work

The old quill weaving of the Canadian Ojibwa showed very fine geometric patterns in which small design units were used. In the early quill and bead embroidery on deer skins both geometric and floral patterns were delicately worked out. Fine quills from the young porcupine and moose bristles were used in these exquisitely embroidered patterns on skins. Small, fine line designs were also used in the etching and carving on wood.

It is generally conceded that the Ojibwa introduced the curvilinear pattern into the western region adapting and embellishing it according to their own fancy.

The Ojibwa made some use of the double curve motif, which was common to all Algonquin tribes. The double curve motif consists of two opposed curves rising from a common center or base. It is usually embellished with scrolls and conventionalized leaves, buds, and flowers. Often elaborate bead work designs are built up about the double curve. It has been used to some extent in the ribbon work.

Designs On Birch Bark

Birch bark articles were probably decorated with designs from an early day. The well-worked out geometric and curvilinear designs on birch bark containers were large, in response to the surface to be covered, and were adapted to the shape of the articles. Floral designs on birch bark were stiff

Plate 78.

Plate 79.

OJIBWA DESIGNS. FROM YARN BAGS

Plate 80.

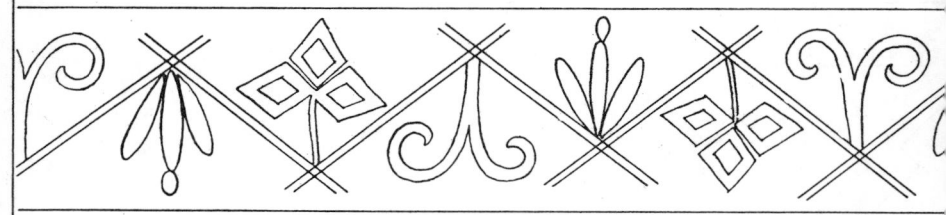

OJIBWA QUILL DESIGNS

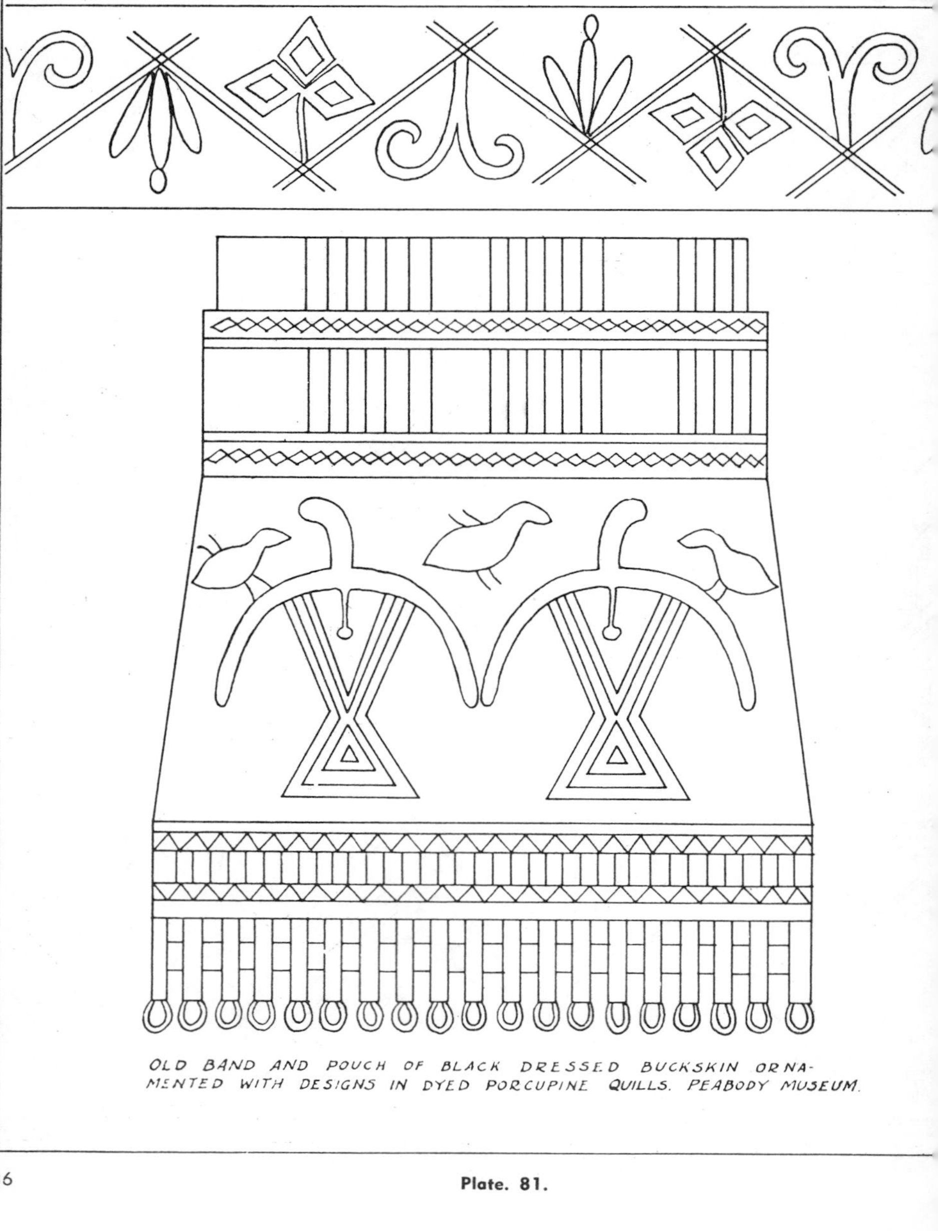

OLD BAND AND POUCH OF BLACK DRESSED BUCKSKIN ORNAMENTED WITH DESIGNS IN DYED PORCUPINE QUILLS. PEABODY MUSEUM.

Plate. 81.

and heavy in their adaptation to the rigid medium. Quill work on birch bark also showed heavier designs less delicately worked out than the quill embroidery on the soft skins, though some of the very old birch bark pieces show delicate floral designs done in fine quills or moose hair. (See section on Birch Bark Containers; page 56)

Designs Used In Beadwork

With the practice of bead weaving and the wide choice of colors that beads offered, elaborate geometric designs appeared. A similar development was shown in the designs in bead embroidery patterns which became large and showy as the designs covered wider spaces and as coarser beads of many colors were used. The later floral designs apparently bear no relation to the fine floral designs that had been used in the quill embroidery and in the early bead work, when only very fine beads were used. Special floral designs were worked out for moccasin decoration. The larger semi-realistic designs were used on pouches, breech cloths, vests and other large articles.

The Ojibwa Indians made use of three types of designs in their bead work, the straight line or geometric design, the conventionalized design, and the realistic or floral design.

Geometric Designs. The geometric design has been used in both woven and embroidered bead work. On the woven band, the design runs down the center, or across the band at right angles, or diagonally. In embroidered patterns the narrow geometric design is generally used as a border. Sometimes however the narrow pattern has been repeated many times to fill a wide surface. The early geometric designs were simple, but some of the later ones used on shoulder pouches and broad bands or sashes are quite complicated.

The design units are usually given familiar descriptive names which probably vary with different groups of craft workers.

The straight line or "running" design is made up of one straight line of beads usually in white against a background of color, if embroidered, or in color, against a white background if woven. Sometimes several straight lines of beads, parallel to one another, were used, each in a different color.

In embroidery work, the running stitch was sometimes varied by using an interrupted straight line, where the unbeaded open spaces were of equal length with the beaded portion of the line. Today this is popularly called the "jumping" design.

A row of beads in contrasting color was sometimes used diagonally across the band. As with the running design, several diagonal lines, each in different color, were sometimes used. The "diagonal" design was formed by one narrow row of beads, or by several rows of beads forming a wide band.

Plate 90.

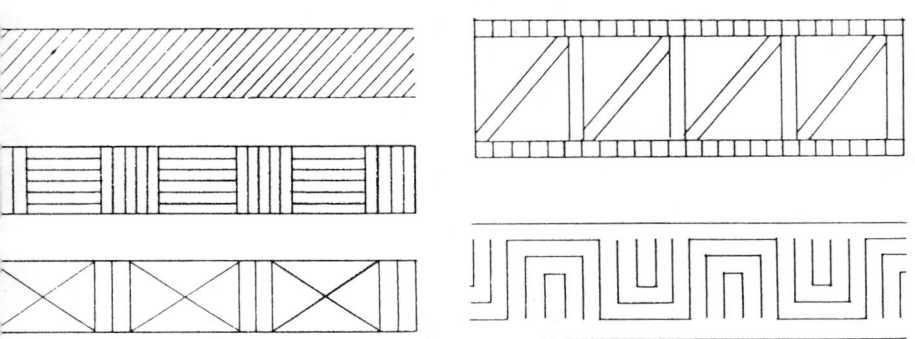

OJIBWA DESIGNS USED ON BIRCH BARK

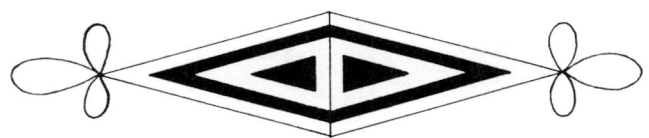

DESIGN FROM THE HANDLE OF A WAR CLUB

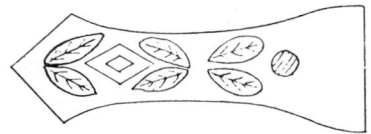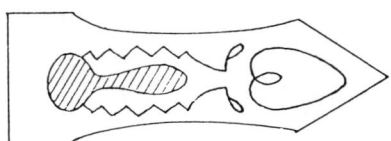

DESIGNS FROM OLD SPOONS

Plate 83.　　　　　　　　　　　　　　　　　　139

The underground panther of the Ojibwa

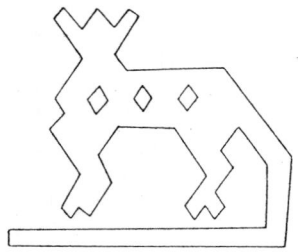

as represented on a nettle fiber bag

 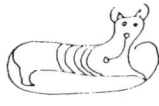 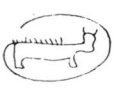  

as engraved on birch bark

The thunder bird of the Ojibwa

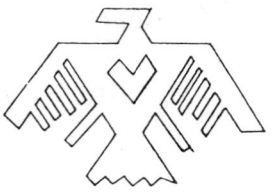

on a nettle fiber bag

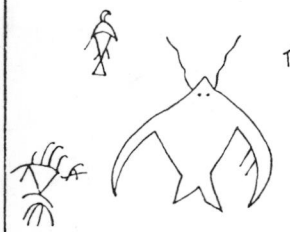 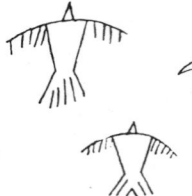   

on birch bark scrolls

Plate 85. 141

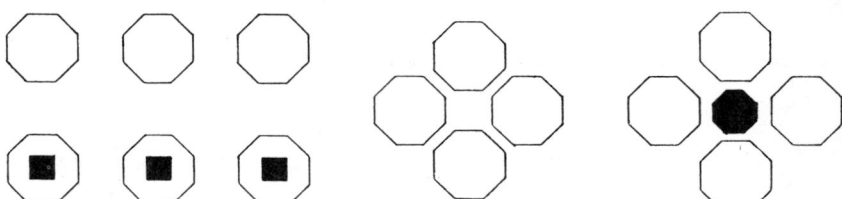

Round bead or dot design   Four dot design

Conventionalized rose design

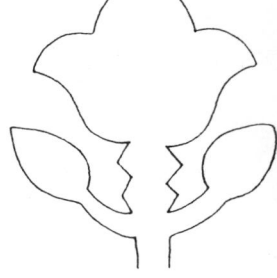

Flower with buds

Conventionalized leaf designs

142   **Plate 86.**

PINE CONE

FEATHER

ROSE

ELK'S HORN

RABBITS FOOT

SPEAR HEAD

BUD

CRABS FOOT

Plate 87.

143

The "zigzag" or "lightning" design, made up of a row of connecting equivalent angles, was commonly used by the Ojibwa Indians in both woven and embroidered bead work.

A double zigzag design, with the lines parallel, called the "skating" design has long been one of the characteristic Ojibwa designs. The name was probably given in later years after the introduction of the winter sport.

Two zigzag lines, opposed to one another, formed the "diamond" design. The "triangular" design and the oblong "block" design were also used as border designs.

Probably the most popular of the Ojibwa designs was the "otter-tail" design, said by the old women to represent the track left by the otter when it crossed the ice in the spring. The typical "otter-tail" border consists of narrow elongated hexagons with two, three, or four diamonds connecting them, the vertical width of the hexagons and the diamonds being the same.

The otter-tail design has been much used on narrow chains and as a border around the yoke and across the straps of the broadcloth dress early worn by the Ojibwa women. To fill in wide spaces, the otter-tail design has been repeated many times in various combinations producing effective patterns. The otter-tail design has been used by the Iroquois and all the lake tribes. It is an old weaving design and may have come to the Ojibwa from their eastern neighbors.

Conventionalized Unit Designs.   In contrast to the continuous border or band designs, so characteristic of the early Ojibwa bead embroidery and weaving, are the isolated or single unit designs used chiefly in the bead weaving. These unit designs have been used alone or in combination with the border designs, and are to be found incorporated in many of the complicated geometric patterns. The unit design appears to have been developed from some object in nature which has been conventionalized by the beadworker as she developed her pattern.

The eight-sided dot, known as the "round bead" design, often done in two colors, is one of the oldest designs used by the Ojibwa in their woven bead work.

A grouping of four dots, with or without a fifth dot in the center is frequently used and is known as the "four dot" design.

Diamonds and elongated hexagons are used alone or combined as in the otter-tail design, in both woven and embroidered bead work. The eight pointed star and the scroll or whorl design occurred in many patterns.

The "conventionalized rose," which may have developed from the four-dot design, is one of the best known Ojibwa designs. It is much used in woven bead work in combination with geometric designs in more or less elaborate patterns.

144

"Leaf designs" were used in many forms both natural or semi-realistic and conventionalized. Realistic maple, oak, and wild grape leaves showing veins as well as outlines were popular as designs on birch bark baskets and in embroidered and woven beadwork patterns. In bead work, the leaf was usually worked out in two shades of the same color, a lighter shade being used for the veins than the body of the leaf. Two leaves were sometimes placed side by side on a band or sash with the colors alternating as they were repeated. Sometimes single large leaves were worked out one above the other with the stems placed diagonally to connect them. Even in the semi-realistic designs, the leaves often become highly conventionalized. Frequently they were used as a background for flowers. Berry, grape, and other fruit designs were used with both natural and conventionalized leaf patterns.

As the leaf gradually became conventionalized in weaving, a rhomboid unit in different sizes and arrangements was used to make up a variety of leaf patterns. The rhomboid also served as the basis for many other unit patterns and borders. Two rhomboids, placed with their acute angles meeting, formed a wing design. Eight rhomboids with their acute angles meeting in a common center, formed a rosette. Border designs were made by arranging rhomboids on the two sides of a central line or stem. Two rhomboids in different colors, placed opposite one another or alternately at short distances and repeated the length of the border, formed popular border patterns.

In addition to the conventionalized floral patterns, made up of flowers and leaves, there are other conventionalized designs that occur frequently in woven bead work. The old "feather" design has been worked out in many different arrangements on both broad and narrow bands. Among the Wisconsin Ojibwa the "cranberry" design has been woven into an elaborate pattern. "Grape" patterns are common. One of the most interesting and apparently most popular designs is the "claw" design, that appears in the later bead weaving. Acquaintance with the crawfish, abundant in the lake region, would explain the incorporation of such a design into their patterns whether or not any special significance could be attached to it.

Semi-realistic or Floral Designs.   Semi-realistic and floral designs have been used in the embroidery patterns of the Ojibwa since prehistoric times. Floral designs are found engraved on birch bark, carved on wood, and used in the patterns on old pieces of moose hair and porcupine quill embroidery. In the earlier work delicate floral patterns predominated. During later years, probably through European influence, a new semi-realistic style developed. The flowers and leaves lost their delicacy and became larger. They were designed to fill the large spaces on the front of bandoliers, on the ends of breech cloths, and on the sides of leggings. As a usual practice the large

146   Plate 88.

floral designs were used on the various parts of the man's costume. They have also been used on some of the later velveteen dresses for women.

The designs most commonly used include rose buds and large, double roses, four-petalled flowers, harebells or blue bells, lilies, morning glories, grapes, maple and oak leaves, pine cones, gourds, and acorns. Of these the large rose and the maple leaf seem to have been the most popular among the Ojibwa. Flower pots and jardiniers, undoubtedly copied from the French, appear in some of the later designs.

Much apparent liberty was taken in the arrangement of the floral designs and with the combination of colors in which they were worked out. Roses were used with grapes and oak leaves. Buds, flowers in full bloom, and fruit were all represented as coming from the same stem. If against a black cloth or velvet background, the stems were usually embroidered in white beads. On some of the very old pieces the stems were decorated with thorns. Though no consistent arrangement is apparent there may have been a few guiding principles that controlled the development of the patterns.

The spot or couch stitch used by the Ojibwa was especially effective in embroidering the floral designs. In the early work, before beads were plentiful, the design was outlined with only one or two rows of beading and the center was not filled in with beads; later the leaf or flower was filled in solidly with row after row of beading following the curved outline of each motif. In many cases the leaves and flowers are of two shades of one hue, several rows being done in beads of a light shade and the remaining rows being filled in with beads of the same hue in a darker shade.

Though the Ojibwa were quick to develop new designs in response to the change in the medium in which they worked they also showed a fondness for the old designs, repeating them in the new medium. Thus the otter-tail design is found in patterns on woven bags, on birch bark containers, in quill and bead weaving, and in embroidered bead borders and bands. The rhomboid design was used on woven mats and bags, in bead and quill work, and in the engraved patterns on birch bark. The conventionalized rose and the eight pointed star have been used in yarn weaving, in bead weaving, in rag rugs, and in birch bark decorations. Each Ojibwa craft article tends to show familiar tribal characteristics reminiscent of the early days.

Cut-out Designs or Patterns. In the old days the Ojibwa women usually tore or cut out a birch bark, raw hide, or proper pattern for the floral motifs which they expected to use in their all-over embroidery work. Cut-out patterns were also used in the ribbon work or applique. An old bladder bag filled with patterns of leaves, roses, and other flowers is a treasure much prized by the collector, and a woman will seldom part with her carefully collected patterns. They are among the most personal of her possessions from

Plate 89.

which only death may separate her. A few well-filled bladder bags are found in museum collections.

When a large design is needed, the cut-out design motifs are taken out of the bag, selected ones are tried in various arrangements until the result is pleasing to the worker, then the pattern is marked on the velvet by dipping a straw or other finely pointed stick into a stiff paste of flour and water, following the outline of the birch bark or paper designs. Curving stems are usually added to unite the leaves and flowers. As the moist flour can be easily removed, any error in the pattern can be quickly corrected. Even when the flour is dry all traces of the outline can easily be removed when no longer needed. Charcoal was also used to mark the patterns. A thin, flat piece of bone, three or four inches long by one inch wide, with smooth, round edges, or a stiff fish bone was used as a pencil to follow the cut pattern on leather, where it left a mark not easily erased.

Bitten Patterns—Birch Bark Biting (Ojibagonsigen). Origin of the cut-out patterns is thought to go back to the "toothwork" or old bitten patterns which the Ojibwa women marked on birch bark with their teeth before modern implements for cutting were available. The designs presented are imitations of flowers, fancy baskets, and human figures. When a pattern was to be cut, the thin piece of bark was folded in two or more folds and a series of dots was impressed on the bark with the eye teeth, the biting process being continued until the dots formed the desired design. The folding of the bark caused a duplication of the design giving symmetrical or balanced patterns and making possible the development of the double curve motif. The practice of preparing bitten patterns extended from Newfoundland to the Plains.

Today only a few old women are skilled in the preparation of bitten patterns. Choice specimens of the birch bark patterns or transparencies are to be found in the museums. (See pages 48 and 95.)

Plate 90.

USE OF COLORS

THE colors secured by the Ojibwa from their native dyes and chosen in the beads and ribbons for their weaving, embroidery, and ribbon work were based on the intermediate hues in many shades. They did not make use of the primary colors as did the Sioux and the other Plains Indians. The hues found in the Ojibwa craft work include red, yellow, green, and blue. Bright red was not used by the old craft workers. Red when used was of a very dark or very light shade. Red violet was popular. Blue violet was also much used. Browns and tans were often combined with lemon yellow and gold. Brown and a light rose were another popular combination. A deep yellow orange was combined with a light yellow orange. Bright orange color was not used by the Ojibwa.

Three shades of the same hue are often found on one piece of bead work. Three shades of green and three shades of blue were much used. As many as twenty-five different colors or shades are to be found harmoniously combined on one piece of bead embroidery.

Black was little used in craft work until black velveteen began to be used as a background. A very dark blue and a very dark green closely approached black and provided the dark shade necessary in some patterns. White beads formed the background of many of the woven and solidly embroidered beaded patterns. Beads of light rose and light yellow were also used for backgrounds. White beads were often used as stems when a floral pattern was embroidered against black velvet.

Though tans and browns predominated in the woven yarn bags and mats, brighter colors were introduced when available. The use of ravelings from red blankets and the redyeing of other old materials indicate the effort which the women made to secure the bright colors. Porcupine quills were dyed in many hues. Soft shades were secured in great variety from the native dyes.

In the Minnesota Archaeologist for April 1942 (Vol. VII, No. 2, Minnesota Archaeological Society, Minneapolis, Minn.) three studies of Ojibwa arts and crafts by Burton Thayer are included. Carefully worked out drawings in black and white serve as illustrations. The titles of the articles are as follows:

"Black" as a Preferred Color in Ojibwa Art.

The Algonquian Trait of Asymmetry in Ojibway Art.

A Comparison of a Few Tribal Pipe Bags.

In these articles attention is called to the early use of black buckskin by the Central Algonquian and the frequent occurrence of black beads. broadcloth, and velvet in the later craft work of the Ojibwa.

Thayer has found that asymmetry is present in many of the Ojibwa patterns—the design on the two sides of a wool bag or on the ends of a band differ. The color of the beads used on the two ends of a band differ, or the colors used on the two moccasins in a pair differ.

The use of welt seams in finishing bags and moccasins is spoken of as a woodland trait. Four ear-like flaps at the top of an Ojibwa pipe bag and a single plain fringe at the bottom frequently occur.

NATIVE DYES

THE Ojibwa women made intelligent use of the rich vegetation in which their country abounded to develop dyes which contributed to the beauty of their craft work. The roots, buds, leaves, flowers, berries, and seeds of plants and the roots, juice, twigs, branches, and bark of trees have been used by them in preparing dyes. Combinations of two or more plant or tree products were often necessary to secure the desired shade. Plants were gathered, dried, and stored to be used when dyes were desired.

Wood ashes, special clays that were found around springs, and other mineral substances were also used in preparing the dyes, usually in combination with some of the plant products.

In the preparation and application of the dye a long process of boiling was often necessary. Simple boiling of the materials to be dyed in a decoction of the dye plant was the usual method employed. After boiling, the bath was allowed to cool and the dyer then rinsed the material in water to remove the unfixed dye. With some materials and dyes the processes had to be repeated a second time. At times a different color was resorted to. The darker shades were secured by reboiling the materials or by allowing the material to stand in the dye for some time. In some cases the work of dyeing continued for as long a period as two weeks or a month.

Colors were set by the use of mordants, one plant being used for the color, while another plant or a mineral substance was used to set the color. Red or black mud, grindstone dust, and water in which iron had rusted served as mordants for some dyes. Many of the colors were fugitive. Others retained their brilliancy for years.

The following is a brief list of plants used by the Ojibwa in the preparation of their dyes.

Alder [Alnus incana var. Americana Regel]—the inner bark was used with bloodroot, wild plum, and red-osier dogwood to dye porcupine quills red and yellow.

Blood root or red puccoon [Sanguinaria Canadensis L.]— the root was used with other plants to dye porcupine quills red; the fresh root was used to color wooden implements yellow.

Bur oak [Quercus macrocarpa, Michx.]—the inner bark was used with hazel burs, butternut bark, and earth to dye porcupine quills black.

Butternut [Juglans cinerea L.]—the root was used with hazel bark to dye rushes black. With the inner bark a brown dye was secured.

Cedar Red [Juniperus virginiana var. crebra Fernald and Griscom]— the inner bark was used alone or with other plants to color the strips of cedar for mats red (mahogany).

Chokeberry [Prunus virginia L.]—the inner bark was used to secure a red dye.

Dogwood, Red-osier [Cornus Stolonifera Michx.]—the inner bark was used with birch, oak, and cedar bark ashes to dye porcupine quills red.

Gold thread [Coptis greenlandica (Oeder) Fernald (C. trifolia (L.) Salisb.)]—the root was used to dye porcupine quills yellow.

Hazel [Corylus americana Walt.]—the inner bark was used with butternut to dye rushes black; green hazel burs were used with bur oak to secure a black dye.

Hemlock [Tsuga Canadensis (L.) Carr.]—the inner bark was used with a little rock dust to set the color, to dye porcupine quills and rushes for matting red (mahogany).

Lamb's quarters [Chenopodium album L.]—the whole plant was used to secure a green dye.

Lichens [Usnea barbata Fr. Sched.]—the whole plant was used to dye porcupine quills yellow.

Maple [Acer sp.]—the rotted wood was used to dye porcupine quills purple.

Puccoon [Lithospermum carolinense (Walt) Mac M.]—the dried root was used with ochre to dye porcupine quills red. Also used for face paint.

Sumac [Rhus glabra L.]—the inner bark and pulp of the stalk were used to dye porcupine quills and rushes for matting yellow.

White birch [Betula papyrifera Marsh.]—the inner bark was used with dogwood, oak, and cedar bark ashes to dye porcupine quills red.

Wild plum [Prunus americana Marsh.]—used with blood root, red-osier dogwood, and alder to dye porcupine quills a bright red; with bloodroot alone a dark red was secured.

The skill of the Ojibwa craft workers in the use of dyes is shown by the success with which they dyed materials of many different textures and qualities. Reeds and bull rushes, porcupine quills, basswood, jack pine roots and wool were dyed in great quantities. Different dyes and different treatments are necessary in dyeing each of these craft materials. Rushes are difficult to dye and often require several dippings to secure the desired shade. Porcupine quills were considered easy to dye and retained the colors a long time. With the disappearance of the fine quill work has gone the knowledge of the source and method of preparation of many of the vegetable dyes with which the quills were colored. Aniline dyes, carried by the traders, were early substituted for native dyes, and are today used even for dyeing quills.

CONCLUSION

B ECAUSE of the perishable nature of the materials in which crafts had been carried on and because of an absence of written records little is known of the evolution of prehistoric craft work among the Ojibwa. At no time within the historic period has the practice of the crafts been static, always it has been subject to change as new conditions have influenced the lives of the craft workers.

As the Indians moved from place to place and became acquainted with the crafts of other tribes, changes crept into their tribal crafts. Contacts with other tribes were immeasurably increased after the horse came into use and travel to distant points became frequent.

The new conditions created by the coming of the traders profoundly affected the crafts as new products were made available to serve as materials for craft work, new designs were suggested by the laces and embroideries brought from Europe, and new needs were felt in the homes. Bags woven of commercial yarns followed those of native fibers; beads were substituted for quills; broadcloth and cotton came into use in place of skins in the making of costumes and costume accessories; commercial thread, cord, and dyes replaced those of native origin. The new materials necessitated the development of new techniques. New design patterns were worked out or adopted in order to used the new materials effectively.

The transfer of education from the home to school deprived the girl of the opportunity to learn the crafts from her mother or grandmother as had been the practice at an early date. The later generations have been less thoroughly trained in the crafts than were their grandmothers and great grandmothers who had developed skill in craft techniques in early childhood.

Changed conditions of living have taken many of the Ojibwa women outside the home to work for their economic support, and to help in the support of their families and they have had little time for bag weaving and rug making.

The present day use of the automobile has increased travel and social visiting has cut into the long hours formerly available for carrying on the slow processes involved in good craft work.

The limited use of craft articles in the Ojibwa home of today has taken away much of the incentive to production. Lack of a well-established market has discouraged the craft worker who has wished to sell her articles. The tourist demand for cheap articles has tended to lower the standard of craft work.

In spite of the many changes within the tribe and in the Ojibwa homes, the love of the craft articles has been kept alive by a few faithful workers who have continued to practice many of the old techniques. They know the native craft materials which were being used when Nicolet visited Sault Sainte Marie in 1634 as well as the later techniques that new materials have demanded. It is from them as well as from the rare old pieces that are to be found in museum collections, that our present day knowledge of native designs and native techniques has been secured.

BIBLIOGRAPHY

Armstrong, Benj. G. and Wentworth, Thos. P.
Early Life Among the Indians.
Press of A. W. Bowron, Ashland, Wis., 1892.

Baraga, Frederic (Bishop)
A Grammar and Dictionary of the Otchipwe Language explained in English. Part I Otchipwe—English. Part II English—Otchipwe.
Printed for Jos. A. Hemann. Cincinnati, Ohio. 1853. Also Beauchemin and Valois, Publishers, Montreal, Canada, 1878, 1880, 1882.

Barbeau, Marius
Assomption Sash.
Bulletin 93. Anthropological Series No. 24. National Museum of Canada. Ottawa, Canada. 1939.

Barrett, S. A.
The Dream Dance of the Chippewa and Menomini of Northern Wisconsin.
Vol. I, Article 4, pp. 254-291, Milwaukee Public Museum, Milwaukee, Wisconsin. 1911.

Bushnell, David I., Jr.
Native Villages and Village Sites East of the Mississippi.
Bulletin 69. Bureau of American Ethnology, Washington, D. C. 1919.
Ojibwa Habitations and Other Structures.
Annual Report. 1917. pp. 609-618. Smithsonian Institution, Washington, D. C.
The Various Uses of Buffalo Hair by the North American Indians.
American Anthropologist, N. S. Vol. XI No. 3, pp. 401-425. 1909.

Carter, B. F.
The Weaving Technic of Winnebago Bags.
Vol. XII, New Series No. 2. January, 1933. Wisconsin Archeologist. Wisconsin Archeological Society, Milwaukee, Wisconsin.

Davidson, Daniel S.
Snowshoes.
Memoirs of the American Philosophical Society. Vol. VI. Philadelphia, Pa. 1937.

Densmore, Frances
Chippewa Customs
Bulletin 86, Illus. Bureau of American Ethnology, Washington, D. C. 1929. Out of Print.

Chippewa Music.

Bulletin 45. 12 plates. 8 text figures. Bureau of American Ethnology, Washington, D. C. 1910. Out of Print.

Chippewa Music II.

Bulletin 53. 45 plates. 6 text figures. Bureau of American Ethnology, Washington, D. C. 1913. Out of Print.

Study of Chippewa Material Culture.

Miscellaneous Collections. Vol. 68. No. 12, pp. 95-100. Smithsonian Institution, Washington, D. C. 1918.

Uses of Plants by the Chippewa.

44th Annual Report. Illus. Bureau of American Ethnology, Washington, D. C. 1927. (Available Govt. Printing Office, Washington, D. C.)

Denver Art Museum, Indian Leaflet Series, Denver, Colorado.

Leaflet No. 22—American Indian Tobacco.

Leaflet No. 36—The Ojibwa or Chippewa Indians.

Leaflet No. 58—Indian Basketry.

Leaflet No. 59-60—Indian Cloth-Making. Looms, Technics, and Kinds of Fabrics.

Leaflet No. 62—Design Areas in Indian Art.

Leaflet No. 63—Indian Vegetable Dyes. Part I.

Leaflet No. 67—Basketry Construction Technics.

Leaflet No. 68—Basketry Decoration Technics.

Leaflet No. 71—Indian Vegetable Dyes. Part II.

Leaflet No. 73-74—Plains Beads and Beadwork Designs.

Leaflet No. 81—Tribes of the Great Lakes Region.

Leaflet No. 85—Tribal Names. Part II.

Leaflet No. 87—Indian Basketry East of the Rockies.

Donaldson, Thomas

The George Catlin Indian Gallery in the United States National Museum.

Smithsonian Report. 1885. Smithsonian Institution, Washington, D. C., 1887.

Douglas, Frederic H. and d'Harnoncourt, René

Indian Art of the United States.

Museum of Modern Art. New York, N. Y., 1941.

Gilmore Melvin R.

Some Chippewa Uses of Plants (Medicinal, dietary, and as dyes).

Michigan Academy of Science, Arts, and Letters. Vol. XVII, pp. 119-144. 1932.

Hilger, Sister M. Inez

Indian Women Making Birch Bark Receptacles.
Indians at Work. Sept. 15, 1935. pp. 19-21. Bureau of Indian Affairs, Department of the Interior, Washington, D. C.

A Social Study of One Hundred and Fifty Chippewa Indian Families of the White Earth Reservation in Minnesota.
The Catholic University of America Press, Washington, D. C. 1939.

Some Phases of Chippewa Material Culture.
Anthropos. Vol. XXXII. 1937. Tanning hides. p. 780. Making birch bark receptacles. p. 782.

Hoffman, W. J.

The Midéwiwin or "Grand Medicine Society" of the Ojibwa.
Seventh Annual Report, pp. 143-600. Illus. Bureau of American Ethnology, Washington, D. C. 1891.

Jenks, A. E.

Wild Rice.
Nineteenth Annual Report, Part 2, pp. 1013 - 1137. Bureau of American Ethnology, Washington, D. C. 1902.

Jones, Volney H.

A Chippewa Method of Manufacturing Wooden Brooms.
Michigan Academy of Science, Arts, and Letters, Vol. XX, 1934. pp. 22-30. 3 plates.

Notes on the Preparation and Uses of Basswood Fiber by the Indians of the Great Lakes Region.
Michigan Academy of Science, Arts and Letters, Vol. XXII, 1936, pp. 1-14. 2 plates.

Some Chippewa and Ottawa Uses of Sweet Grass.
Michigan Academy of Science, Arts, and Letters. Vol. XXI, 1935. pp. 21-31. 2 plates.

Kinietz, W. Vernon

The Indians of the Western Great Lakes, 1615-1760.
Chippewa pp. 317-338. University of Michigan Press. Ann Arbor, Michigan. 1940.

Kohl, J. G.

Kitchi-Gama (Big Water), Wanderings Around Lake Superior.
Chapman and Hall. London. 1860. Canoes, pp. 27-37. Snow Shoes, pp. 332-337.

Lismer, Marjorie

Seneca Splint Basketry.
Branch of Education Bureau of Indian Affairs, Washington, D. C., 1941.

McKenney, Thos. L. and Hall, James.

History of the Indian Tribes of North America.

3 volumes. D. Rice and A. N. Hart, Philadelphia, Pa. 1854.

Biographical sketches and portraits of principal chiefs.

Mallery, Garrick

Pictographs of the North American Indians.

Fourth Annual Report. 1886. Bureau of American Ethnology, Washington, D. C. 1887. pp. 199, 200. Plate LXXXIII.

Picture-writing of the American Indians.

Tenth Annual Report. 1888-89. Bureau of American Ethnology, Smithsonian Institution, Washington, D. C. 1893.

Mason, Otis T.

Aboriginal American Basketry.

Annual Report 1902. pp. 374, 375, 385, 386. Plates 121, 122, 131, United States National Museum, Washington, D. C.

Aboriginal Skin Dressing.

Annual Report 1889. pp. 553-589. Plates LXI-XCIII (Scrapers). United States National Museum, Washington, D. C.

Michelson, Truman

Article on Meaning of "Ojibwa."

Miscellaneous Collections. Vol. 78. No. 1. Smithsonian Institution, Washington, D. C., 1927

Mooney, James

Chippewa.

See Bulletin 30. Handbook of the American Indians. Vol I. pp. 277-280. Bureau of American Ethnology, Washington, D. C. 1907.

Morgan, L. H.

Houses and House Life of the American Aborigines.

Contributions to North American Ethnology. Vol. IV United States Geological Survey. Washington, D. C. 1881.

Orchard, William C.

Beads and Beadwork of the American Indians.

Contributions. Vol. II. Museum of the American Indian, Heye Foundation, New York, N. Y. 1929.

The Technique of Porcupine Quill Decoration.

Among the North American Indians, Vol. IV. No. 1. Museum of the American Indian, Heye Foundation, New York, N. Y.

Reagen, Albert B.

The Bois Fort Chippewa.

The Wisconsin Archaeologist. New Series. Vol. III. No. 4. pp. 101-132. Sept. 1924.

Picture Writings of the Chippewa Indians.
The Wisconsin Archaeologist. New Series. Vol. VI. No. 3. pp. 80-83. June 1927.

Schoolcraft, Henry R.
The American Indians, Their History, Condition, and Prospects, From Original Notes and Manuscripts.
New Edition. Rochester, N. Y. 1851.

Skinner, Alanson
The Culture Position of the Plains Ojibway.
American Anthropologist. New Series. Vol. XVI. 1914 April to June. pp. 314-318.

Smith, Harlan I.
An Ojibwa Cradle.
The American Antiquarian. Vol. XVI No. 5. September, 1894, pp. 302, 303.

Smith, Huron H.
Botanizing Among the Ojibwa.
Yearbook, 1923. Vol. III, pp. 38-47. Milwaukee Public Museum, Milwaukee, Wisconsin.

Smithsonian Institution
Study of Chippewa Culture.
Smithsonian Miscellaneous Collections. Vol 68. No. 12. pp. 95-100.

Speck, Frank G.
The Double Curve Motif in Algonquin Art.
Memoir 42, Illus. Canadian Department of Mines. Geological Survey, Ottawa, Canada, 1914.
Montagnais Art in Birch Bark, A Circumpolar Trait.
Indian Notes and Monographs, Vol. XI, No. 2, 156 pp. 4 figures, 24 plates. Museum of the American Indian, Heye Foundation, New York, N. Y. 1937.
The double curve motif and cut-out patterns are shown.

Thayer, Burton
Black as a Preferred Color in Ojibwa Art.
The Algonquian Trait of Asymmetry in Ojibway Art.
A Comparison of a Few Tribal Pipe Bags.
Minnesota Archaeologist. Vol. VIII, No. 2. April 1942. Minnesota Archaeological Society, Minneapolis, Minnesota.

Waugh, F. W.
Canadian Aboriginal Canoes.
The Canadian Field-Naturalist, Vol. XXXIII. May 1919. Reprint August 11, 1919. Geological Survey, Ottawa.

Weltfish, Gene
> **Prehistoric North American Basketry Techniques and Modern Distributions.**
> American Anthropologist, Vol. 32. No. 3. 1930. pp. 454-495.

Winchell, N. H.; Hill, Alfred J.; Brower, Jacob V.; and Lewis, Theodore H.
> **The Aborigines of Minnesota.**
> The Minnesota Historical Society. The Pioneer Company, St. Paul, Minnesota. 1911.

Wissler, Clark
> **Indian Beadwork.**
> Guide Leaflet No. 50. Illus. American Museum of Natural History, New York, N. Y. 1931.
> **Indian Costumes in the United States.**
> Guide Leaflet No. 63. Illus. American Museum of Natural History, New York, N. Y. 1931.

Plate 91.   Reed doll.

PLATES OF OJIBWA DESIGNS

	Plates	Pages
Bag designs	92- 98	163-169
Quill design	99	170
Band, belt and sash designs	100-118	171-189
Cut-out designs	119	190
Applique designs	120-124	191-195
Moccasin designs	125-126	196-197
Beaded pouches	127-132	198-203
Bead embroidery	133-145	204-216

KEY TO COLORS USED IN OJIBWA DESIGNS

1. Dark green
2. Light green
3. Dark red
4. Pink, rose, or light red
5. Blue
6. Light blue
7. Deep yellow or orange
8. Yellow
9. Violet or purple
10. Light red or violet
11. Black
12. White (used as background)
13. Tan
14. Brown
15. Grey
16. Amber

OJIBWA DESIGNS FROM A WOVEN BAG 100 YEARS OLD

Plate 92.

163

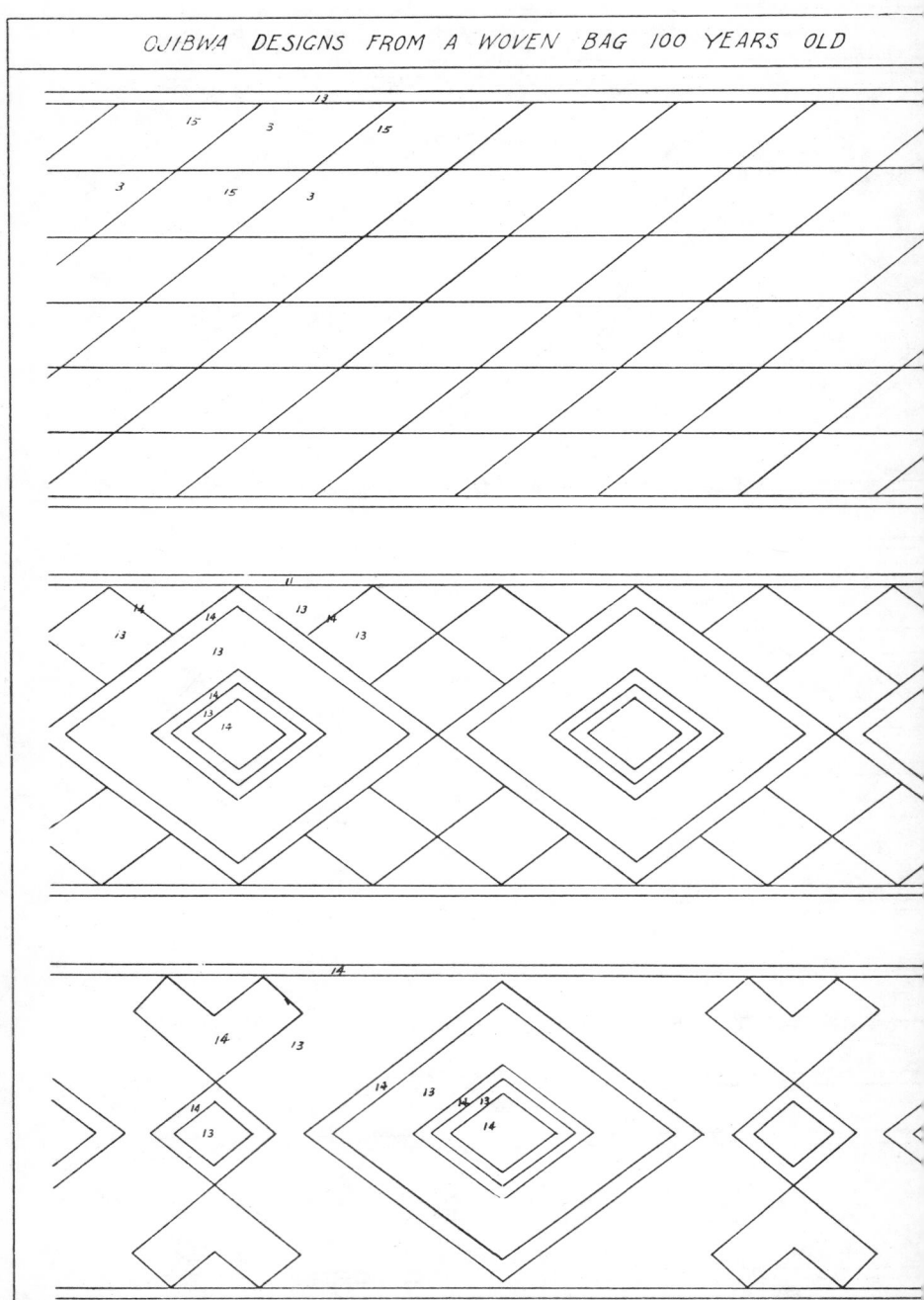

OJIBWA DESIGNS FROM A WOVEN BAG 100 YEARS OLD

Plate 93.

OJIBWA DESIGNS FROM WOVEN YARN BAGS

Plate 94.

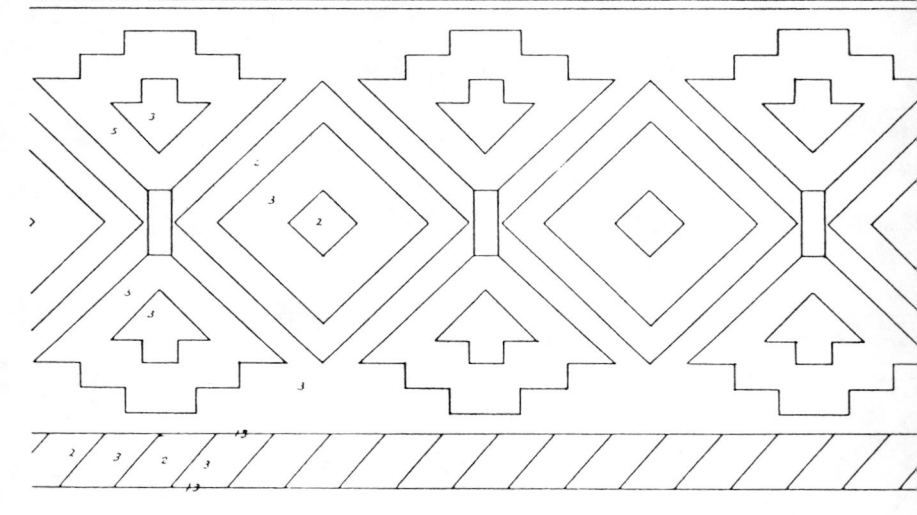

Plate 95.

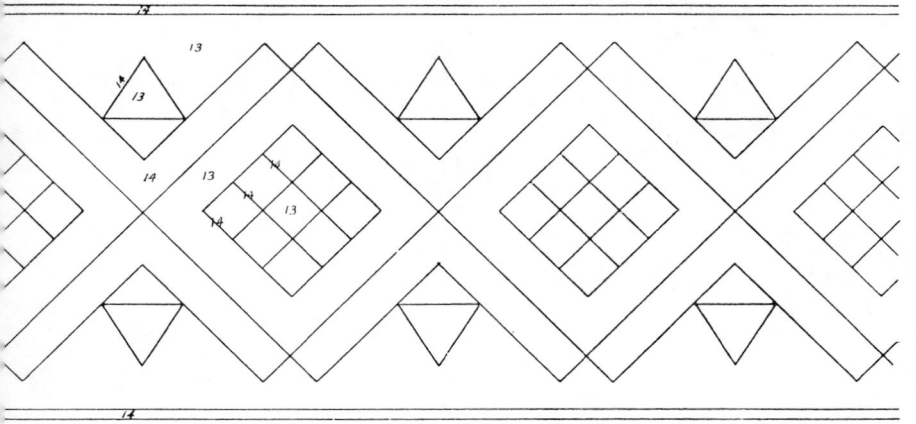

Plate 96.

Plate 97.

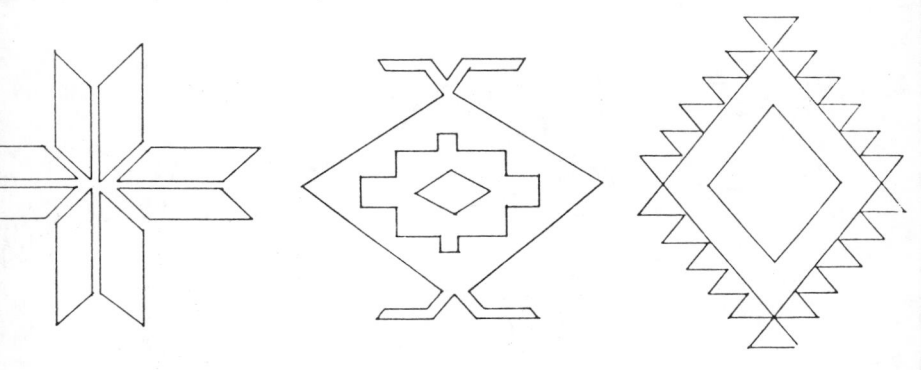

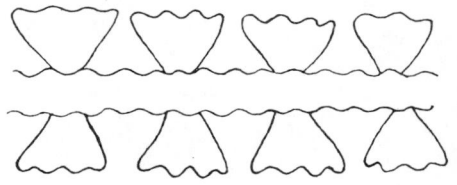

Plate 98.

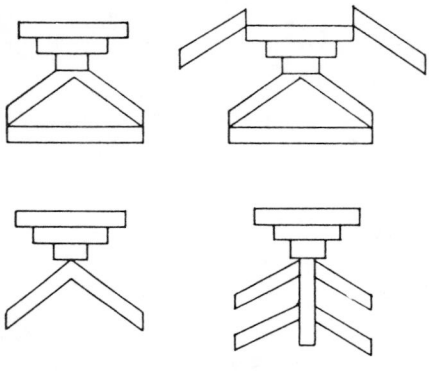

VERY OLD THUNDERBIRD DESIGN

DOUBLE CURVE DESIGN
DONE IN QUILLS

AN ALL OVER DESIGN
DONE IN QUILLS.

Plate 99.

OJIBWA DESIGNS FROM BEADED SASHES (WOVEN)

CLAW DESIGNS (CRAW FISH)

Plate 100.   171

OJIBWA DESIGNS FROM BEADED SASHES (WOVEN)

GREEN BAY

172

Plate 101.

Plate 102.

174

Plate 103.

FEATHER DESIGNS

Plate 104.   175

Plate 105.

OJIBWA BEADED GARTER DESIGN

Plate 106.

OJIBWA DESIGNS USED ON BEADED BELTS

Plate 107.

OJIBWA DESIGNS USED ON BEADED BANDS

Plate 108.

179

OJIBWA DESIGN DONE IN VERY FINE BEADS ON A SILK
BACKGROUND ON A WOMAN'S LEGGINGS

RIBBON WORK ON THE SAME LEGGINGS

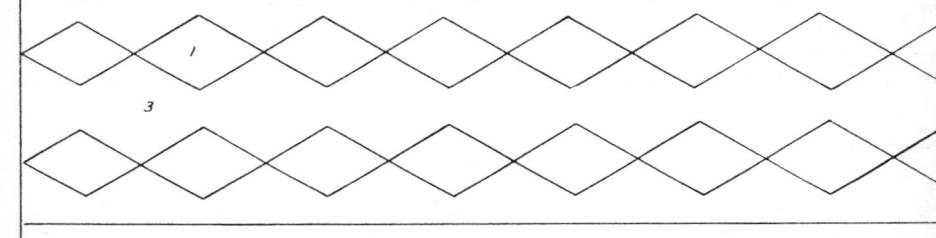

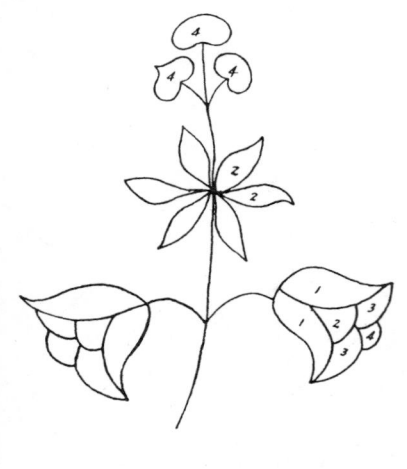

BEADED DESIGN ON A BAG

SCROLL DESIGN USED IN THE
BEADWORK OF THE RED LAKE INDIA

Plate 109.

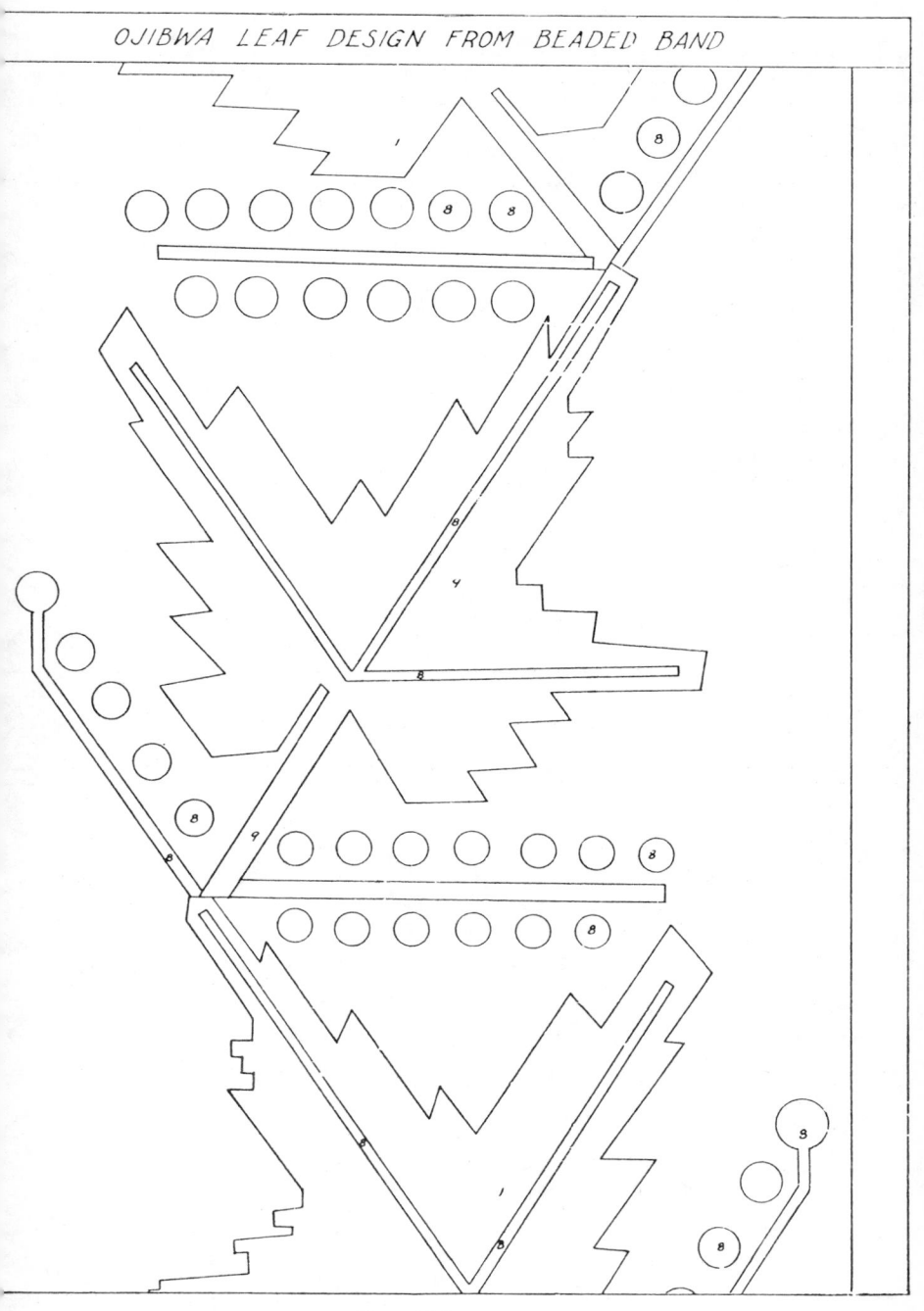

OJIBWA LEAF DESIGN FROM BEADED BAND

Plate 110.

181

OJIBWA BANDS (VARIATIONS OF THE CLAW DESIGN)

Plate 111.

OJIBWA DESIGN FROM BEADED BAND

Plate 112.

183

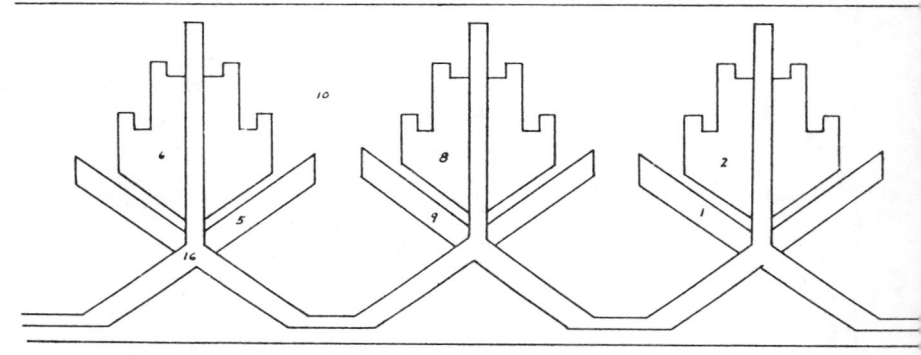

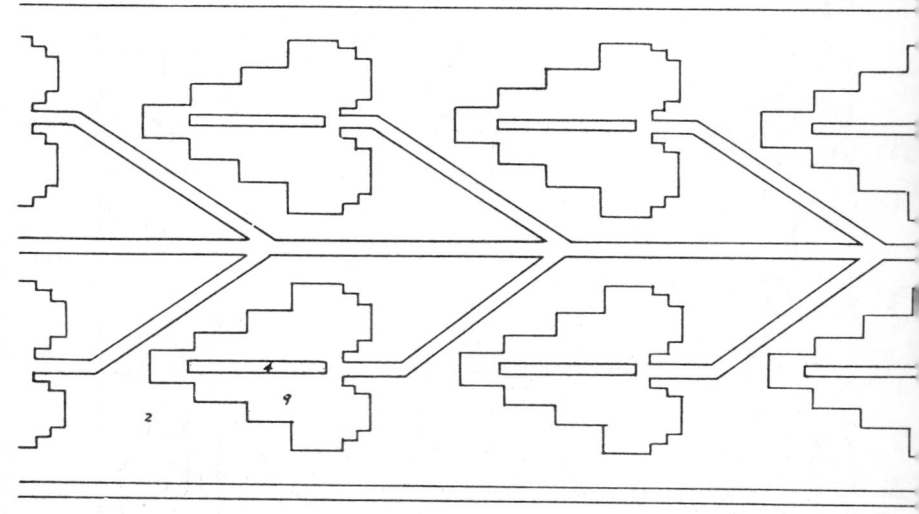

Plate 113.

Plate 114.

OJIBWA DESIGN FROM BEADED BAND

Plate 115.

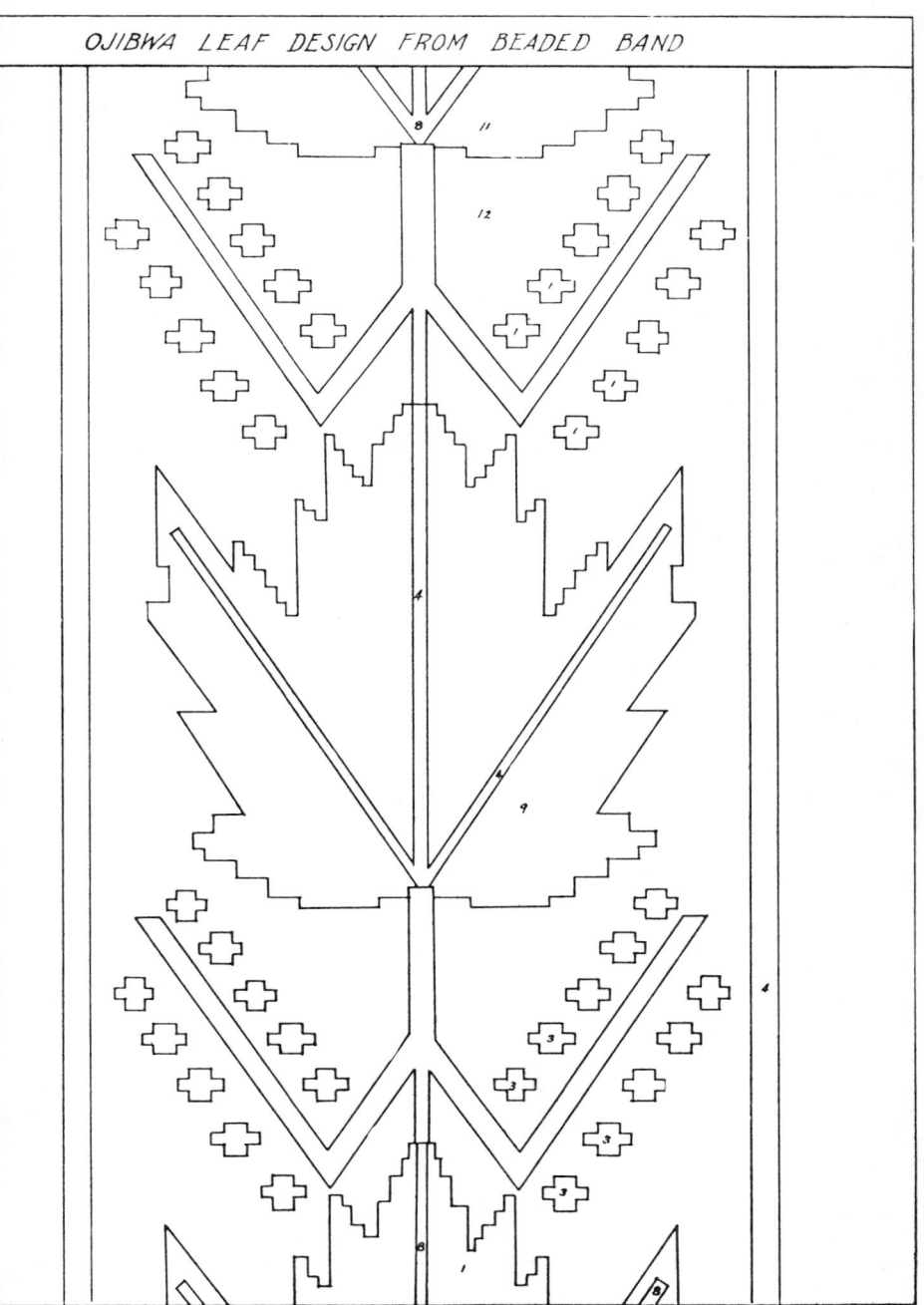

Plate 116.

OJIBWA DESIGNS USED ON BEADED BANDS

Plate 117.

Plate 118.

189

Plate 119.

OJIBWA APPLIQUE DESIGN.   ST. PAUL

DESIGN FROM WOMAN'S LEGGINGS.   OUTLINE IN VERY FINE BEADS ON SILK BACKGROUND

Plate 120.

Plate 121.

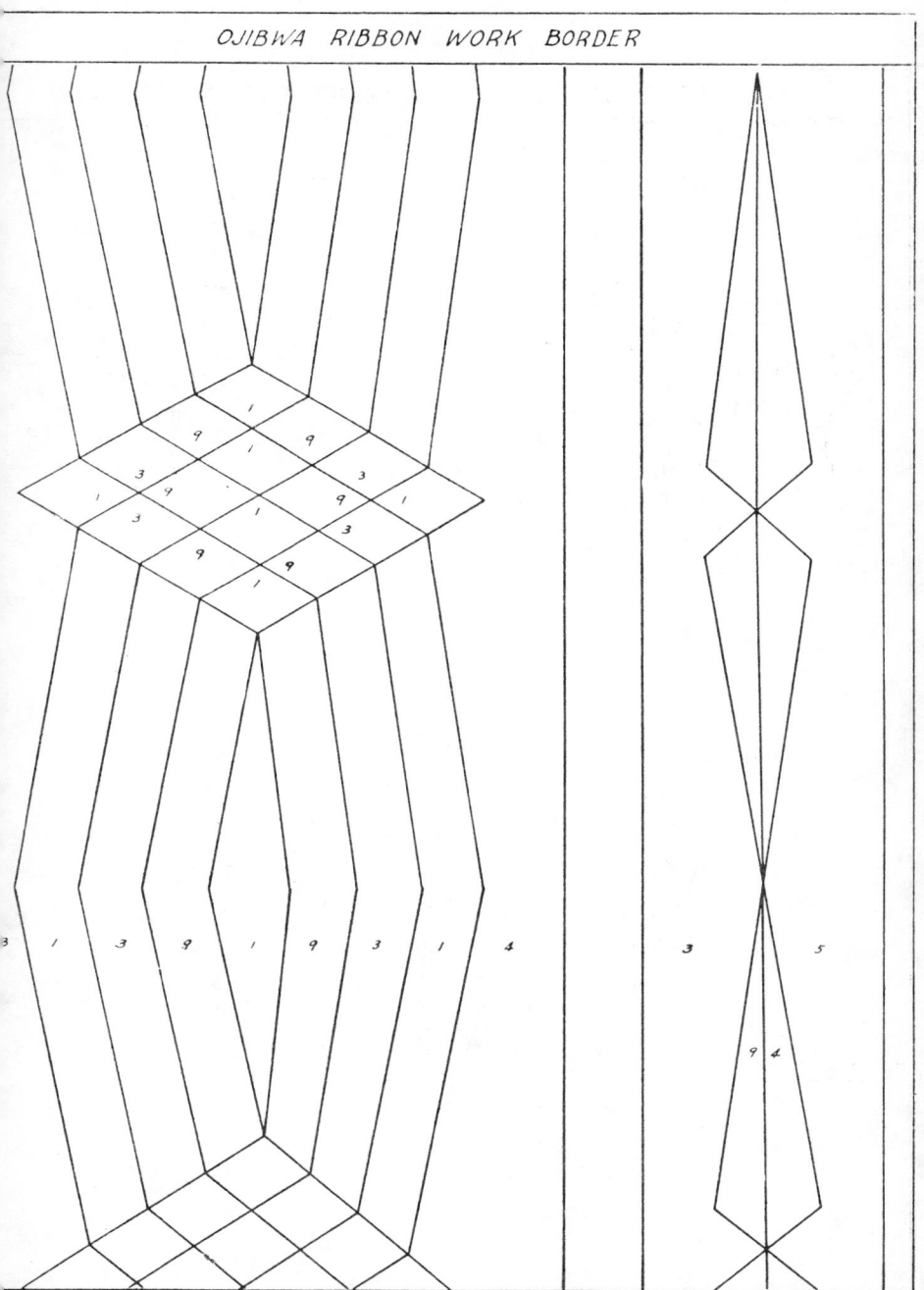

Plate 122.

Plate 123.

Plate 124.

Plate 125.

Plate 126.

Plate 127.

Plate 128.

Center

Plate 129.

Plate 130.

OJIBWA BEADED POUCH DESIGN (IN PART). ST. PAUL.

Center

Plate 131.

Plate 132.

Plate 133.

Plate 134.

Plate 135.

Plate 136.

Plate 137.

Plate 138.

OJIBWA DESIGNS USED IN BEADWORK

Plate 139

Plate 140.

Plate 141.

Plate 142.

Plate 143.

Plate 144.

OJIBWA DESIGN USED IN BEAD EMBROIDERY IN MANY COLORS

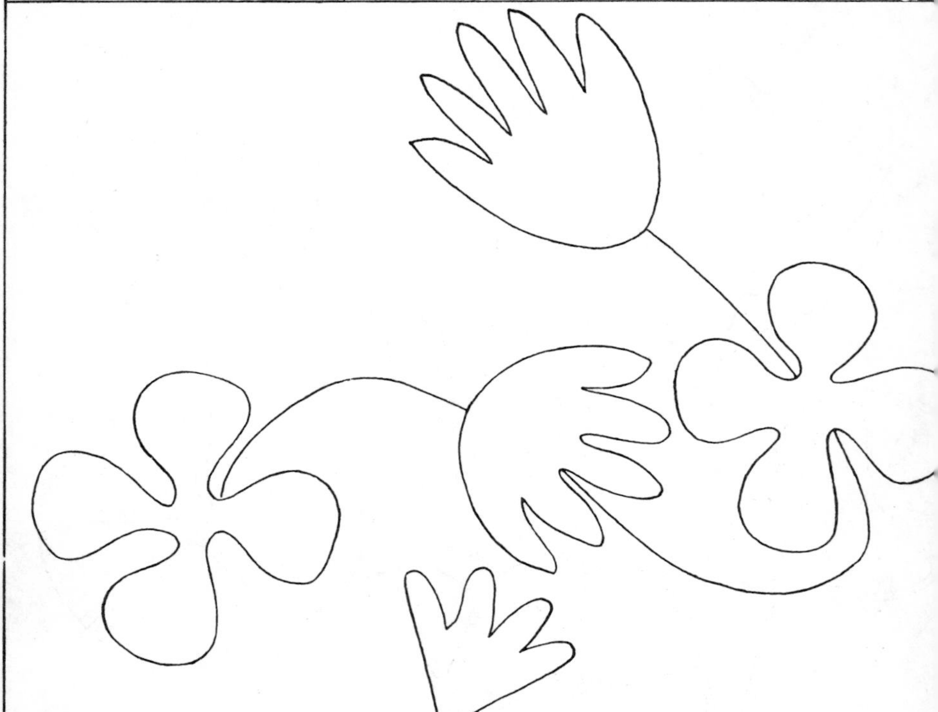

Plate 145.